Lost Restaurants of DENVER

Robert & Kristen Autobee

AMERICAN PALATE

Published by American Palate
A Division of The History Press
Charleston, SC 29403
www.historypress.net

First published 2015

ISBN 978-1-5402-1177-4

Library of Congress Control Number: 2014953329

Contents

Acknowledgements   5

Introduction   7

1. All the Delicacies of the Season: Denver Dining from
   the Fifty-Niners to the Gilded Age   13
2. The Regular Places and *Madre* and *Otosan* Find Homes   41
3. An Order to Go: Rockybilts, Horribleburgers, and the Enigma of
   North Denver's Canoli   63
4. Migrating Tastes: Denver Goes Metropolitan   81
5. "Every Day the Curtain Goes Up": Denver in Search of Its
   Own Tune, 1970–1990   113
6. The Check Please and Where Do We Eat from Here?   135

Notes   145
Index   155
About the Authors   160

Acknowledgements

The authors wish to recognize and thank everyone who spoke to us in the course of this project. Their enthusiasm and thoughtfulness remind us that food is often the first course of building friendships. The encouraging words, helpful suggestions, time, and expertise of the librarians, archivists, and curators at the Denver Public Library, Western History Department, and History Colorado were invaluable. We appreciate the comments and perspectives of Dr. M. Frisbee and Dr. L. Lohman.

We also wish to remember Robert and Ruth Mohr for their kindness and hospitality that live on in their sons and grandchildren.

Finally, special thanks to our mothers and fathers, who showed us what silverware to use and taught us to always thank our host when invited out for a meal.

Introduction

A city is more than its architecture or its sports teams. It is what its residents cook and eat. In a time when most conversations revolve around two topics—what people saw on television the night before and what they recently ate—dining keeps us in touch with others and gives a community its character. Now and in the past.

The ground rules for this dining history of Denver are brief. This story is of Denver's "lost" restaurants through the owners, the clientele, and the food they served. We hope that this will include a warm memory of a good meal or two. But why did we write about a restaurant that lasted only a few years in an off-the-track neighborhood, while a long-standing institution receives barely a mention? Allow us to say the following: the buffet was too big. This volume acknowledges some of the city's heralded restaurants while recognizing the trends, groups, and special dishes not discussed in previous examinations of this subject.

The number of restaurants recalled by and to the authors was staggering. How many Denverites remember the Club Sheik Araby on 1027 Broadway; the Organ Grinder on Alameda; Valente's on West 38th Avenue in Wheat Ridge; Grandpa's Hamburger Haven, also on West 38th; the Holly West; the Peppermill; the Gemini; Wuthering Heights; Cocos; Little Pepina's; the revolving restaurant on the top floor of the Holiday Inn overlooking Colorado Boulevard; Baby Doe's Matchless Mine; Mattie Silks; the Bay Wolf; or the Rocky Mountain Diner?

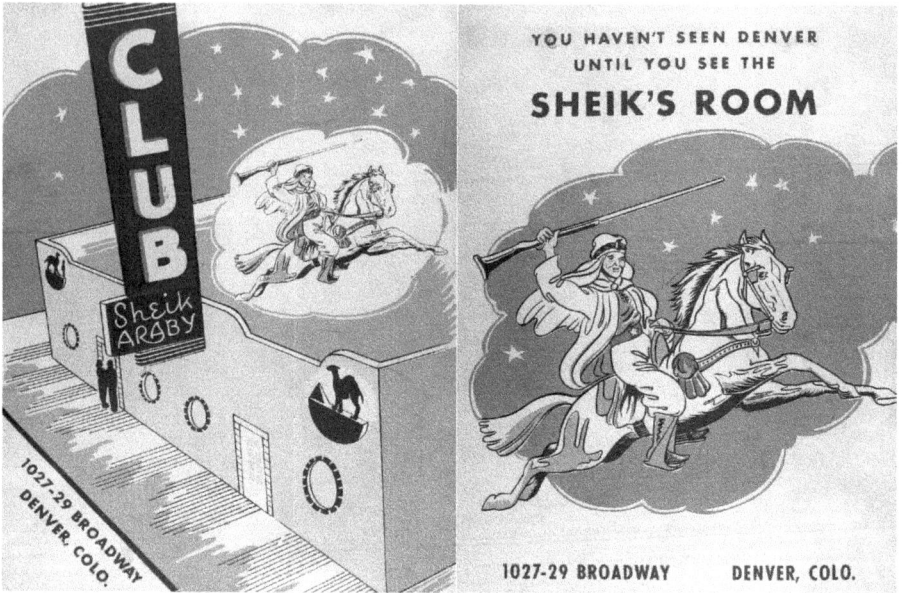

It wasn't the Thief of Broadway, but the Club Sheik Araby is one of thousands of Denver restaurants from the past 150 years. *From Menu Collection, WH1509, Western History Collection, Denver Public Library.*

Congratulations are in order for Patsy's Inn in north Denver for being a few years short of a century. The Fort in Morrison has championed late owner Sam Arnold's vision of Wild West cooking for more than fifty years. Now forty, Casa Bonita shows no signs of waving the white sopapilla flag of surrender. We wish we had space to tell the story of the El Rancho in Evergreen or Eddie Bohn's Pig 'n' Whistle on East Colfax in Denver. Each place remembered—or forgotten—no doubt had stories deserving of a multivolume set.

This history of the Mile High City through its restaurants is a story of "red sauce" restaurants in north Denver, Mexican combination plates served out of people's kitchens, African Americans denied service by the city's established restaurants, and partnerships formed between ethnic groups that celebrated being alive through delicious food. It is also the story of an isolated yet growing city with self-esteem issues in search of recognition as a "destination." Veteran food critic John Lehndorff is well aware that the city's contributions to the national dining scene had a touch of absurdity: "Initially, Denver was a joke—Denver Omelets and Rocky Mountain Oysters. Things changed with the arrival of people and trends. Now there are dozens of good bakeries, craft beers, ciders, and chocolatiers."[1] Despite the municipality's lingering inferiority complex, the turn in this tale is that Denver has had some pretty good places to eat all along.[2]

Today's clichés were not even catch phrases when a rush of ne'er-do-wells came to the banks of Cherry Creek during the late 1850s. The colorful image of the mining camps of Denver and Auraria, filled with men who "squat and ate beans and jerky,"[3] soon gave way to a bustling outpost that could boast of an ice cream parlor as fancy anything you would visit in Chicago or St. Louis. At least that was the implication in the mining camp's only newspaper, the *Rocky Mountain News*.

The town's first business directories strongly indicate that the first Denverites were more drinkers than diners. Saloons outnumbered places to eat by ten to one throughout Denver's first two decades. Newspaper accounts, letters to eastern homes, and diary entries show that there was a better chance at finding bad home-brewed whiskey than good home-cooked meals. Mrs. Samuel Dolman should be credited as Denver's first female restaurateur, as she sold pies to hungry miners tired of their own cooking. Mrs. Dolman used her earnings to build a boarding house. In Denver and elsewhere on the frontier, the men who left their families behind while they looked for work or gold ate at the house or hotel where they lived.

By the late 1860s, a pair of French *frères*—Fred and Louis Charpiot—introduced continental delights on Lawrence Street between 15th and 16th. When history and hot meals meet on the printed page, more often than not, the maître d' is French diarist Marcel Proust. Americans might recognize the author of *À la Recherché du Temps Perdu (In Search of Lost Time)* as a reference in a food magazine article or book that drifts back to a recollection of a great tuna sandwich or a five-course meal. Proust probably never consulted an atlas to find Denver. Nevertheless, a contemporary, Louis Simonin, came to Denver in 1867 and wrote that a restaurant operated by one of his countrymen rivaled the *boîtes*, or cafés, that Paris had to offer.

At the same time, and a few blocks from Charpiot's Hotel and International Restaurant, Chinese immigrants served whites and other Chinese along "Hop Alley" in Denver's Chinatown, before a race riot wiped most of it from the city in 1880. African Americans ran restaurants downtown and, increasingly, in the Five Points neighborhood by the close of the century. African American James Cole should be remembered as Denver's first "celebrity" chef. In other cases, the town grew so fast that stereotypes got in the way of making money or a good meal. Or so the African American women who ran their own restaurants could attest.

Early in the city's dining story, a lack of self-confidence darkened its view of its restaurants when compared to other cities. In 1883, William E. Murphy of Murphy's Restaurant stated, "Colorado has no typical, original food to set before the connoisseur." Murphy observed that Colorado "is composed of people from the corners of the earth." A contemporary "women's guide" entitled *The Rocky Mountain Cook Book* had "not a single recipe" of Colorado origin. The book contained New England Dinner, Virginia Baked Ham, Baltimore Egg Nog, and even Philadelphia Scrapple. It took a while, but only a tablespoon of Denver's restaurants would eventually earn a degree of respect east of the Great Plains or west of the Rockies. Eventually, the diversity created the well-respected Denver palate.[4]

Between the dawn of the twentieth century and the Second World War, the city boasted several noteworthy restaurants. Pell's Oyster House, The Manhattan, Bauer's, and The Edelweiss Café were pillars of Denver dining. Like the city itself, they were not too fancy, but they were respectable and guaranteed a good meal reasonably priced. Concurrently, Denver's hamburger stands, chop suey joints, chili (or sometimes chile) parlors, and Mexican restaurants provided cheap and (for the time) somewhat exotic alternatives to what the "Big Four" offered every day.

One troubling reality of this history reveals that Denver's restaurants were a stage for racism. There is scant scholarly research about the contributions and lives of the city's African Americans in the culinary world. The Manhattan, the most celebrated restaurant of its day, excluded African Americans from 1903 until it closed in 1941. Denver's ethnic cuisines receive little recognition as they relate to the study of the north side's Italians and Mexicans, Five Points' African Americans, and the Japanese along Lawrence and 20th Streets.

Denver's history is neither cosmopolitan nor chaotic. Racism, prejudices, acceptance, and perceptions influenced restaurateurs' decisions about menus and diners' choices of patronage. This prairie outpost respected French culture, and French expatriates opened restaurants serving their own dishes. The Chinese arrived in 1869 and were universally reviled and relegated to specific neighborhoods almost immediately. It took twenty-five years before they advertised their restaurants to whites. Restaurants and neighborhoods were segregated, but the occasional examples of cultural mélange include the Chinese restaurant in Five Points that served both Americanized Chinese and soul food as early as the 1930s.

When the Japanese began settling in around 1910, the few restaurants that attracted more than fellow countrymen served what was expected, the

Chinese-American hybrid chop suey. Similarly, it was Greeks, not Mexicans, who first popularized chili. During the Second World War, Italian American restaurant owners added southern fried chicken to their menus to avoid having their patriotism questioned. For all the camels and pyramids on the 1940s Sheik of Araby's 187-item menu, the most exotic dishes were anchovy cocktail and chicken ravioli.

Restaurants, like a living thing, struggle to find their way, come into their own, and possibly know some success before eventually leaving the scene as tastes change. Such was the case for the "Big Four" by the close of the Second World War. As service members returned or made new homes here, the location of the city's restaurants, and the types of food on offer, expanded. As others arrived from places deemed more refined, a new generation of restaurants featuring Americanized versions of European, or continental, cuisine came forward. Lafitte's, the Normandy, and, of course, Pierre Wolfe's Quorum brought the promise of haute cuisine, celebrity, and dishes that Denver had never seen or tasted.

Similar to amusement parks, a few restaurants from the 1960s and 1970s—the Yum Yum Tree, 94th Aero Squadron, and the eternal Casa Bonita—have or had similar branches somewhere beyond the Rocky Mountains. Even the fondly remembered Denver Drumstick began in west Texas before imprinting itself on the memories of Denverites over fifty.

Not as well documented as other regional or neighborhood specialties, the Mile High City had its own hamburger, the Rockybilt. For a city of mostly newcomers, the Rockybilt lingers in the memories of many residents even though the chain sold its last sack of hamburgers in the early 1980s. To this day, homesick newcomers tarnish Denver's civic self-worth. In a 2013 example, Denver city council member Albus Brooks campaigned for the In-N-Out hamburger chain to establish an outpost west of the I-5. Brooks is a transplant from California, and he wants a taste of home.

The rise of Denver's suburbs may have added "metropolitan" before the city's name, but it built an invisible wall around the city and its established, familiar restaurants. Families spoke of being afraid of going downtown and their preference for what their suburb had to offer.

Some (mostly transplants to the Mile High City) would say that a history of Denver dining has to be brief. It's true that because of its location, Denver's culinary history is always a few paces behind the trends and innovations found in the kitchens of New Orleans, San Francisco, and New York. An honest gourmand would admit that another stereotype—the prevalence of beef on many of Old Denver's restaurant menus—still hangs on.

Introduction

The people of Denver, like the residents of other midsize metropolises, spent the last half of the twentieth century and the first two decades of this century fighting to either save or bury the unique local elements, relying on heritage tourism, or avoiding the smear associated with the term *provincial*. The dining pendulum is swinging back toward greater self-worth through use of local ingredients grown by producers who care about their crops. The Denver dining scene, like other cities west of the Mississippi, will never be as self-contained as it was a century ago. However, the sense of "local is better" has taken root.

Survival unites the cafés, nightclubs, dives, and restaurants mentioned in this book. The lucky ones beat the slim odds in a business where few succeed for very long. The following chapters discuss the groups, the families, the gimmicks, and the resignation when it was time to move on. In the end, death, taxes, or family infighting forced the heroes and heroines of this history to turn the cardboard sign over to "Closed" one last time.

Now, please consult that increasingly rare, but always necessary, research tool: the phone book. Now, turn to *R* for "restaurant." No, you are not in need of an eye test. The phone book reflects the explosion of restaurants across metropolitan Denver. In the 2010s, tracking the number of Denver restaurants—whether in the phone book or spread across the metro area—is truly a blur. The Denver restaurant scene of the early twenty-first century has cuisine choices from places many Denverites could not locate on a map forty years ago.

Currently, Denver may be in the middle of its most creative age as a restaurant town. However, we didn't get to where we are today without a few good meals. If you pronounce the name of Denver's original restaurant row "*lara*-mer" instead of "*lair*-mer," if you like your green chili the approximate color of a Broncos home jersey, and call a chunk of sausage wrapped with chile pepper inside pizza dough a canoli instead of a calzone, then you will find much to remember.

CHAPTER 1

All the Delicacies of the Season

DENVER DINING FROM THE FIFTY-NINERS TO THE GILDED AGE

First, there was prospecting. After mining, supplying miners, keeping saloons and hotels, running restaurants was an early Denver occupation. The miners, prospectors, cowboys, and mountain men have a well-documented reputation of coming to town for whiskey. We read little about the attempts of these rough, weather-beaten men to find a hot cooked meal. Most weren't "rode hard and put away wet" until they got to Colorado. Jim Baker—army scout, early frontiersman, and non-cook—subsisted on venison. He roasted ribs by bracing them with a stick, bone side to the fire. These ribs fit nicely in his saddlebags, and he would eat them until the meat began to spoil. Then he would go hunting again. This way, Baker hunted and cooked every two or three days.[5] Cheap whiskey in the next town sounds pretty good.

In the mid-nineteenth century's wide-open West, travelers on horse or by stage were at the mercy of the mile house's common table. By 1859, some nineteen different guidebooks described the beauty and opportunities in the Pikes Peak mining country. These guides indicated the best routes to take, how much to expect to pay for supplies, the last town to buy supplies in, local weather, and geological sights along the way, as well as told a few white advertising lies. Within ten years of Denver's incorporation, the population totaled almost five thousand. There was a growing tourist economy and a healthy restaurant trade.

Homesickness for apple pie or fresh baked bread doesn't make adventurous fireside tales. It is one thing to fry, roast, or boil over an open fire, but baking over a campfire is quite another thing. After the discovery of gold along Cherry Creek, Denver's population was about ten men to one woman. Not all men were bad cooks, and not all women liked or were adept at baking. Isabella Bird visited an Estes Park ranch in 1873 and recorded in a letter home to London, England, "Evans offers me $6.00 a week if I will stay into the winter and do the cooking…I think I should like playing at being 'hired girl' if it were not for the bread-making! But it would suit me better to ride after cattle. The men don't like 'baching,' as it is called in the wilds—i.e. doing for themselves."[6] Miss Bird left the next day for Denver.

Gold, not dreams of new cities, brought men to the banks of the Cherry Creek and the South Platte River. Not finding gold that first summer, and rather than walking, riding a horse, or otherwise making the six-hundred-mile trip back to Omaha, some stayed the winter and intended to prospect again in the spring. Many early pioneers were entrepreneurs by necessity if not temperament. For some, prospecting gave way to city boosterism. A few understood their own and saw opportunity in baking. The bakeries they created were Denver's first freestanding restaurants, not associated with a hotel or saloon. However, some early bakeries did also serve beer or offer lodging.

Denver's start was the completion of General William Larimer's "house" or log cabin in October 1858. At the same time, he and other men laid out a city with streets as wide as eighty feet.[7] By year's end, Edward Karczewsky of Chariton, Iowa, and Henry Reitze of Omaha, Nebraska, had opened Denver's first restaurant, a bakery in a sixteen-foot-square structure on 11th Street between Market and Wazee.[8]

By 1859, Karczewsky & Company had relocated to Blake Street in Denver, built a second bakery on Ferry Street in Auraria, and offered lodging. Today, Auraria is a small Denver neighborhood, but then it was Denver's rival on the other side of Cherry Creek. The *News* noted, "The Above establishments are fitted up in the most approved style and are now prepared to furnish meals and lodgings at all hours and prices to suit the times. Bread, Crackers, Pies, and Cakes always on hand, in quantities to suit purchasers."[9]

Karczewsky and Reitze must have been decent bakers. No small-town business survives on first-time customers. In 1866, J.F. Wharton noted in the city's first history, "[T]he increasing demand for the 'staff of life' prepared by them, soon required more room, and they removed to a more commodious building that they had erected near Wootton's store, on Ferry Street. Their new bakery was built of logs, with a frame front and a shingle roof."[10] Nothing indicates what Karczewsky & Company charged for a loaf of bread, but it would take dried apples, flour, or gold dust in trade.

A pinch of gold dust bought a drink at any saloon, and the barkeeper did the pinching. Mary Dorsey Sanford described using gold dust in Denver in her diary entries during July 1860: "My hens lay every day, and I get…$2.00 per dozen. What money I can get for my eggs is paid in gold dust, the only currency used here. It is carried in buckskin bags or bottles, and is weighed out on small scales. We cannot get a smaller amount than 25 cents of anything. They don't seem to value money much here, especially those who make it easily."[11] For a time, Denver's economy was artificially inflated to a starting point of twenty-five cents—the smallest amount that could be weighed on a scale. However, newspaper ads suggest that gold dust wasn't the only way to purchase food.

Taking raw ingredients like flour in trade is practical for bakers but cumbersome for shoppers. Early settlers and merchants faced hardships to stay supplied, including toad-floating rains, high winds, rough and unmaintained trails, exhausted and thirsty oxen, and, depending on the route and year, aggressive Sioux or Cheyenne Indians. *The Illustrated Miner's Hand-Book* includes a shopping list to outfit four men for six months. Third on the list—after three yoke of oxen (six), a wagon, and cover—is ten one-hundred-pound sacks of flour.[12] Even if they gave up prospecting or didn't find gold, they had a form of currency.

Early Denver bakeries advertised that they accepted dried apples in trade. Dried apples have two roles, first as fruit and second as yeast starter. There are as many types of bread as there are leavening agents. Three common breads, familiar to Denver's early settlers and us, are sourdough, yeast, and quick breads. Historic sourdough starters were equal parts flour and water. Depending on temperature and humidity, they could take between three days and two weeks to be ready for baking. Using additional yeast cuts the time to mature from days to hours and doesn't allow a sour taste to develop. Quick breads use various kinds of salts, sodas, baking powders, or eggs for leavening and are baked immediately after they are mixed.

It is hard to appreciate the "simple" pioneer kitchen. Yeast is made several ways. Apple peels and cores were dried and saved separately as farmers dehydrated the harvest. Rehydrated apples were cooked or baked, and the peels and cores used to make a type of beer. During the beer's fermentation, a yeast-rich froth formed on the surface. The cook used the yeast-froth in bread. So, taking dried apples in trade guaranteed the bakers had apples for pies and the means to make yeast and beer.

Another early business model united baking and brewing, and the Union Bakery Restaurant & Lager Beer Saloon appears to be the first. Henry

Humble and his wife came to Colorado from Utah. Their daughter, Auraria, is a competitor for the title of "first white child" born in Denver. He also advertised in the *Rocky Mountain News* on April 26, 1859, "Corner of 5th & St Louis Streets, Denver, Fresh Bread, Pies, Cakes and Crackers always on hand." Although the Humbles returned to Utah in 1863, this combination of bakery and saloon persisted in Denver throughout the 1880s and included the St. Louis Beer Hall and Restaurant owned by Swiss-born Florian Spalti.

Libeus Barney, who arrived in May 1859, prospected for a few weeks but claimed to find very little of "the dust."[13] Barney returned to Denver two months later armed with a new business plan. After complaining that every third building, log cabin or otherwise, was a "groggery" dealing out whiskey, he decided to build a restaurant and concert hall. He expected to invest $2,000 and have a return of $50 per day "at least til spring." With any luck, spring would bring wagon trains of fresh supplies and new settlers and tourists wanting hot meals and entertainment.

Six months later, Barney wrote, "Stores, hotels, restaurants, etc, of no very mean pretensions, spring into being as if by enchantment." If one form of enchantment was finding gold, another form was running out of cash. It seems foreign but credit was unlikely, unless the borrower could guarantee the loan with something of value like gold. The cashless traveler, or the miner who failed to strike it rich, had to work or sell something of value to raise cash or risk becoming indigent poor. Almost from its beginnings, Denver had a homeless population, pawnshops, and secondhand stores.

Over the summer of 1859, Mr. and Mrs. Samuel Dolman headed for Pikes Peak but were out of cash by the time they reached Denver. Mrs. Dolman reminisced in 1925 that they could not pay the one-dollar ferry fare to move their wagon across the undammed and unrestrained South Platte. She wrote that they had plenty of provisions and a No. 7 Charter Oak Stove. The Dolmans set up camp while they tried to work out their next move. As it turned out, they did not have to move far.

It is not clear how Mrs. Dolman arrived at the idea of selling baked goods, but as a woman cooking in Denver was somewhat of a novelty at the time, her angle was quite simple. A hungry, dusty miner smelled fresh baked bread and bravely started up a conversation. Mrs. Dolman baked bread, pies, and cookies and "sold them out readily for there was so many men that had done their own cooking they wanted a change. I got good prices for my cooking… we soon had a house…the windows covered with canvas…we…made tables and bedsteads and benches to sit on…it was called the Kansas House." The Dolmans would not be the last to fail at prospecting but succeed at baking.[14]

Mrs. Lavina Porter, a Missourian, also kept a diary of her family's migration west. The Porters decided that if they liked the look of Denver, they would stay. If not, they would go on to California. Mrs. Porter's descriptions of Denver in the summer of 1860 are not flattering. She is probably accurate about the cows roaming the streets, and her account agrees with those of other pioneers as to the number of rum shops and the ills caused by drinking. Some of her disgust may be a result of being less entrepreneurial than the Dolmans. The Porters also ran out of cash, and Mrs. Porter got the best price for her wedding crystal by selling it to a saloonkeeper. With the deal made, the Porters were off to California.[15]

"Scarcely a trade or business that belongs to civilization but is well represented here…cabinet makers, jewelers, tailors, restaurants, rum-holes, and hotels, theaters, negro minstrelsy," wrote Libeus Barney in November 1859. Barney wrote his letters home to a newspaper, and it was to his advantage to be a good Denver booster. Still, advertisements in the *Rocky Mountain News* on April 26, 1859, illustrate commercial diversity, even if much of it did revolve around buying and selling liquor or tobacco and renting rooms.

"BACK TO THE BOÎTES AND BOULEVARDS"

[A] *Frenchman has built a café and restaurant here, and at the foot of the Rocky Mountains worthily represents the cuisine of our country. He has also all the wines of France, and the Americans are well acquainted with the path to his place.*

—Louis L. Simonin, Denver, 1867[16]

There is no food critic like a tourist. Moreover, if that tourist was from Paris, France, he probably knew a bit about dining and service. In his letters home, Louis Simonin wrote very little about eating. He marveled at the number of meals served in Barney Ford's restaurant in Cheyenne, Wyoming. He also praised the territory's produce: "[I]n these privileged climates there are such fine vegetables and that in Paris we are served watery foods, fibrous, tasteless, one is truly tempted to import our provisions from Colorado."

Colorado mine owner J.P. Whitney invited Simonin, a well-traveled mining engineer, to visit Colorado. They met at the 1867 International Exposition in Paris. Whitney financed an exhibit of mineral specimens in the hopes of gaining foreign investors for Colorado mines through published reports by scientists. Four years passed before Louis Simonin published his observations along with his letters home.

Despite limited remarks on dining, Simonin is often quoted as saying, "There are no cooks in this country, but everyone is a little religious," and many conclude that Denver lacked good restaurants. Really Simonin was reminding his French readers of the basic difference between the English and the French. Since at least the 1790s, the French have been fond of saying that England has 3 sauces and 360 religions, whereas France has 3 religions and 360 sauces. Charles Talleyrand, a French politician, is said to have remarked, "I found but one dish and thirty-two religions" during a 1790s stay in America. The Americans and English were more concerned with feeding men's souls and the French with feeding men's stomachs.

In the eighteenth and nineteenth centuries, American inns and roadhouses served food, as the French say, *la table d'hôte*, or at the host's table. No menu—guests ate what the host ate. The innkeeper threw whatever was available in a pot and served it whenever someone came through the door. The result probably tasted the same no matter where you stayed. But then "one dish and thirty-two varieties" captures America today, where it seems possible to have a hamburger at any restaurant yet attend different religious services every day of the year.

The Frenchman in the quote was Frederick Charpiot, who arrived in Denver in about March 1861. Charpiot emigrated from France in the early 1850s and was a merchant in Olive, Iowa, where his brothers, George and Louis, farmed. Unlike many early settlers, Frederick Charpiot made several trips back to Iowa and no fewer than four trips back to France. Ships' passenger lists call him a merchant. Why a merchant if he runs restaurants? The *Rocky Mountain News* explained that in July 1866:

> *Fred. Charpiot, The Pioneer Restaurant Keeper of Denver has returned from Europe, and having purchased the International Restaurant of A. Arbour, again tenders his services to the good people of Colorado. His Stock of Wines and Liquors embrace the purest brands and best varieties, being imported by Mr. Charpiot in person. The tables will, at all times, be furnished with the choicest delicacies of the markets.* GIVE FRED A CALL.[17]

Still ten years from statehood, Colorado's largest mining camp could boast French wines imported by a Frenchman.

The Charpiot brothers reunited in Denver in the 1860s. In 1869, brother Louis opened the Capitol, a French restaurant and oyster saloon

Manhattan along muddy Larimer Street. At the Delmonico of the West, Frederick Charpiot kept a cellar of fine wines and more than enough oysters for 1870s Denver diners. *From Western History Collection, X-18546, Denver Public Library.*

at 35 Larimer Street, just west of F Street (today's 1400 block). The *Rocky Mountain News* immediately proclaimed it "the neatest and most elegant establishment of that kind in Denver." Similar to eastern restaurants, the Capitol had "little rooms or stalls, which comfortably seat six persons." The stalls had mirrors and curtains for patrons' privacy. A pair of chandeliers lit the carpeted dining room. The Capitol posted its bill of fare and wine list in the cloakroom at Cole's Dance Hall.[18] Other than nightclubs, it remains difficult to find a good Denver restaurant open after a show.

The Delmonico of the West is probably the best known of Charpiot's restaurants. Opened in 1871, Charpiot named it for *the* Delmonico in New York City. The Delmonico family created a restaurant that eastern tourists recognized for fine food, elaborate dinners, and careful attention to customers and customs. Charpiot hoped to attract business by association. In nineteenth-century Denver, the vacationers were families like the Vanderbilts and Goulds, and celebrities like Buffalo Bill Cody and Oscar Wilde, who dined on oysters, locally sourced game, vegetables, fine pastries, and imported French wines, just like at the Delmonico in Manhattan. Vacationers still look for names they recognize.

Frederick Charpiot died in his hometown of Branges, France, in 1907. Although its gold-lettered sign remained in place, the Delmonico of the West eventually became a warehouse. Demolished to make way for Writer's Square in 1954, few remembered its former glory.[19]

The ways of the Second French Empire inspired mining-camp Denver. "French" was both French and code for "fancy." G. Guiraud advertised "[a]ll kinds of French goods," including dress patterns and embroidery supplies for the ladies. Guiraud's ad also announced "Jewelry for Christmas Presents, Fresh French Vegetables, imported Champaign and Swiss Absinthe." Men still outnumbered women in 1865. Occasionally, a thoughtful husband recognized how hard his wife's life was—surely "French" goods meant more on the lonely prairie. On the other hand, mining and railroad jobs were speculative and attracted single men or married men who left their families back home. Contemporary accounts suggest that many early Denver women displayed questionable morals, and French goods helped set the stage, so to speak. Maybe the presence of these "brides of the multitudes" also encouraged the trade in oysters.

THE *R*s HAVE IT

Ten years before the *Rocky Mountain News* proclaimed Louis Charpiot's Capitol Restaurant "the neatest and most elegant" French and oyster palace in Denver, merchants Clayton & Lowe advertised "New York Goshen Butter, dried peaches and apples, and canned peaches and oysters." Yes, oysters—in a Denver only a few months old.

Parker and Huyett, authors of the 1859 *Miner's Hand-Book* mentioned earlier, included on their shopping lists expected provisions such as flour, sugar, and bacon, plus necessary hardware, guns, clothing, India-rubber goods, and tents. Under the heading of "Luxuries," they included smoking tobacco and pipes, whiskey, "4 cans fresh peaches $3.00, and 12 cans Oysters (Maltby's Best), $15.00."[20]

Oysters were everywhere and done every way a cook could imagine. Because oysters were so popular, so perishable, and not always available fresh, they were one of the first foods to be canned, mass marketed, and shipped nationwide. Nineteenth-century cookbooks, newspaper advertisements, and special event menus presaged Dr. Seuss, as oysters were boiled, broiled,

Restaurateur James Cella promised "Everything First Class" at his oyster house on 15th Street in the 1870s. *From Western History Collection, X-18546, Denver Public Library.*

curried, deviled, escalloped, fried, fricasseed, pickled, raw, steamed, and stewed. There were oyster croquettes, fritters, omelets, and pies. They were served *à la Newberg* like lobsters, roasted on toast, stuffed in poultry, or served with cocktail sauce.[21]

Denver's restaurants served them raw by the pint or quart. Although we found no reference in Denver, eastern establishments sometimes hung lanterns covered with red canvas outside their doors to indicate the presence of the poor little bivalves, as well as to associate them with other red-light districts. The association of oysters with aphrodisiacs, dating from ancient Rome, was firmly entrenched in mid-nineteenth-century America. Many early restaurants did not welcome women without a male escort and provided

Victorian Denver craved the oysters found on either side of the continent. Most bivalves' final shucking came from the hands of Baltimore women. *From authors' collection.*

separate "Ladies Dining Rooms." In a lovely and sly double standard, they provided private rooms, or curtained stalls, in case ladies came escorted or happened to order oysters. An 1892 commentator found ladies "downtown on shopping expeditions usually take a run into Glendinning's, the Chesapeake, Pell's, the Woman's Exchange or cozy places of a like character, where oysters are the feature."[22]

Oysters, although not common, were not as much of a novelty in early Denver as our modern prejudices would consider. On September 1, 1863, Barney Ford's second restaurant, People's Restaurant, advertised that "[g]entlemen will find at all hours his tables supplied with the most choice and delicate luxuries of Colorado and the East. Private parties of Ladies and Gents can be accommodated with special meals, and Oyster Suppers to order in his upstairs saloon…Game of all kinds, Trout, &c., constantly on hand for regular and transient customers, and served up in a style second to no other restaurant in the west."[23] Beyond date night food, oysters were both high-class dining and the poor easterner's food. And like gold dust, oysters' rarity in Denver increased their value and popularity.

Denver's First Celebrity Chef

Barney Ford's first restaurant was a lunch counter in a lean-to attached to his barbershop. When a disastrous early morning fire on April 19, 1863, engulfed his property, Ford rushed his pregnant wife, Julia, and three-year-old son, Louis, to safety from their one-room home behind the lunch counter. Then he went into the street to fight the rampaging fire. The blaze spared Larimer Street, but most of Denver's business district burned, including Ford's business and home. When the embers cooled, Ford borrowed a hat to make a call on the Kountze Brothers Bank for a loan.

Barney Ford dreamed big. He wrote a plan for a two-story building, with furnishings, and bids totaled $9,000. Uninsured, without savings, and with land and barbershop mortgaged, Ford owed more money than he was worth. However, banker Luther Kountze felt that Ford was one of the better risks in Denver and agreed to loan the money at 25 percent interest. People's Restaurant opened on August 16, 1863, with the dining room on the ground floor, a bar on the second, and a barbershop in the basement. Over the next few weeks, ads for his new restaurant announced the arrival of oysters, lemons, and Havana cigars.

A 1907 postcard of the Albany Hotel's Bohemia Room carried a cheery message: "It is good and warm here so I ordered Soup for Dinner, Mamma." *From authors' collection.*

The businesses did well, as it was one of the first to reopen after the fire. Ford repaid his loan with interest ninety days after opening. Ford's biographer wrote, "Thereafter his credit was so good that he had no need of it."[24] By 1864, he was the fourteenth-wealthiest man in Denver. When he retired after creating and selling restaurants in Denver and Breckenridge, St. Louis, Missouri, and Cheyenne, Wyoming, and investing in mines and barbershops, Ford was worth $250,000, and Mrs. Ford was listed in the 1898 *Social Register.* For those not familiar with his story, Barney Ford was a self-educated, runaway slave.

Denver's first decade was challenging for Ford and all who made a living from food and hospitality. The first generation of restaurants competed with boarding houses, hotels, and saloons. In terms of services, it is hard to define differences between frontier hotels with public dining rooms and frontier boarding houses with public dining rooms. A further complication: the word *house* was a common business name or description used by hotels, boarding houses, saloons, and restaurants.

Unlike today, the price of Denver hotel rooms included a meal plan in 1860. The "American plan" often came under rebuke. For the customer, it meant renting a hotel room, prepaying for meals, and then finding out that it was the worst restaurant in the city. For the hotel owner, it made dining room management easier knowing that the number of guests equaled the number of meals to prepare and the amount of food to have on hand.

By 1865, many hotels also offered the "European plan," where guests paid separately for lodging and meals or board. Proprietors "of the different public houses" gave notice on November 8, 1865, that they were unable to furnish board at the current prices.[25] The 1863 fire was the first disaster to impact prices, followed by an even more disastrous Cherry Creek flood the next year. In 1865, Native Americans retaliated against settlers for the military's attacks on their villages and encampments. The Cheyenne and Sioux tribes were briefly successful at disrupting Denver's supply routes. The tribes attacked stage stops and destroyed or delayed shipments from the East. For short periods, wagon trains and stagecoach lines stopped services. Freighters—the men who operated the wagon trains—found it necessary to hire armed guards or ask passengers to be at the ready with their guns. Merchants passed the cost of protecting goods along to the customers through price increases.

There were at least three price tiers in hotels, boarding houses, and restaurants. The highest tier offered lodging and board for $20.00 to $35.00 per week. Transient boarders, those staying less than a full week, paid $4.00 to $5.00 per day. Single meals cost $1.25, and day board (meals only) was $15.00. The second tier offered lodging for $1.00 per night, day board for $14.00 per week, single meals for $1.00, and transient board for $4.00 a day. The restaurants owned by John J. Reithmann and Chas. Whipple & Company offered single meals for $1.25 and board by the week for $24.00. The third tier served meals for as little as $0.25. Tourists could now stay at any hotel and arrange for a week of meals at any restaurant.

Separating lodging from board may seem like a small change. During the 1860s, crafty entrepreneurs developed other options. Carr's Hotel advertised in the 1866 city directory that "[f]reighters and travelers wishing to do their own cooking, will find here a convenient cook house free of charge." The shared cookhouse was located in the hotel's companion business, the Mammoth Corral. Corrals offered stables, livery, and auction services for both goods and stock as needed. The December 31, 1869 *Rocky Mountain News* advertised, "Save money by going to Tarbet's, opposite Elephant auction stand, for a hot mutton pie and glass of beer, or cup of coffee, for 25 cents."

Hotel dining rooms became competitive. They could no longer count on the same number of diners as lodgers. Dining rooms could no longer be an afterthought—what the innkeeper's wife threw in the pot. Now they

The "American plan" was the order of the day in the 1880s. This image of the Metropolitan Hotel's dining room at 16th and Holland (now Market) was likely posed. *From Western History Collection, F-24852, Denver Public Library.*

Staff stands at the ready at the Royal Restaurant at 1641 Curtis Street. The Royal served Denver's hungry office workers of the early twentieth century. *From authors' collection.*

required separate business models, with their own unique financial risks. If one restaurant refurnished its dining areas to the latest eastern styles, others would follow suit. Hotel dining rooms competed in food quality, service, and amenities. The era of the celebrity chef and owner had arrived.

Just Who Is in the Kitchen?

In July 1867, Frederick Charpiot advertised his new French restaurant on Blake Street as "having secured the services of two of the very best cooks in this or any other country the public may rest assured that the good name and custom heretofore given the proprietor will be satisfactorily sustained." While the ad doesn't name names, this is one of the earlier ads to brag about the cooks.[26]

Whether the claim was legitimate in A.C. Clark's New Restaurant advertisement of July 21, 1866, no longer matters. The restaurant at the corner of the today's Blake Street and 16th Avenue advertised:

> *This neatly fitted house is now open and ready to serve up the best that the market affords, in the Best Style of the Art. Mr. James Cole, than whom there is no better cook in the west, will have charge of the culinary department. This, in fact, is sufficient recommendation for the house. We promise to keep a FIRST CLASS HOUSE in a first class style. Meals served at all hours, Day or Night.*[27]

Nearly 150 years later, James Cole leaves us with questions, not answers. We don't know where he learned to cook, where he built his reputation, or where he was born. His listing in the 1866 and 1880 city directories reads, "Cole, James (col) cook." Denver city directories listed most African Americans as either "col.," "cold," or "col'd." Beyond this, all we know about Cole, as he managed to avoid even the federal census takers, is that he lived on Holladay Street between G and H Streets (today's 1600 block of Market Street).

Between 1858 and 1866, three classes of restaurants emerged, and Denver moved from finding its daily bread to dining on the offerings of the best cooks. By the mid-1860s, Denver's population had started to settle in with the arrival of tradesmen, families, wives, children, and tourists. Into the 1870s, two French restaurants, and their fancy wines, competed for diners with expendable income, and Denver was ready for dessert.

BAUR'S CANDY MOUNTAIN

Otto Baur built a local institution on sugar, eggs, and chocolate. In 1867, Baur came west with experience as a confectioner in Ohio and New York. His first job in Denver was at the first bakery, City Bakery. After a few failed starts at running his own business, Baur and his business partner, James Colwell, rented a store at the corner of 16th and Lawrence for baking and catering in 1870. Within a year, Baur had created a drink of ice cream, fruit juice, and seltzer water subsequently known as an ice cream soda. News of this confection spread across the country like wildfire and established Baur's reputation nationally. Sugar-fueled ambition led to Baur's 1891 move to 1512 Curtis. His nephew, Joe Jacobs, took over operations after Otto's passing in 1904. Jacobs added a restaurant in 1918, a bakery at 16th and Glenarm, and a branch in the May Company Store. Eventually, Baur's ventured past

Baur's china offers a glimpse of refined dining from the nineteenth century. *Accession #2013.77.18.1, History Colorado, Denver, Colorado.*

the Cherry Creek and opened a store in the new Cherry Creek Shopping Center and, finally, one in Lakewood during the 1950s.

It's Baur's Restaurant on Curtis Street that people remember. With its marble soda fountain and white-and-gold candy and pastry counters, it resembled "an altar in a neoclassical temple." Baur's *pièce de résistance* was a sixteen-layer pound cake with chocolate or jelly separating the layers. For birthdays, customers could have a chocolate pound cake iced to look like a telegram with the recipient's name and the sender's message scrolled in icing.

A columnist with the Denver weekly *City Edition* recalled in the 1980s, "The nicest present you could possibly give some extra special person…was a half-pound box of Baur's Almond Mija candy."[28] Baur's is gone, but its amazing Mija Pie will still make somebody happy.

Mija Pie

1 cup sugar
4 tablespoons cornstarch
¼ teaspoon salt
2 cups milk
2 egg yolks
4½ tablespoons cocoa
2 ounces Baker's German's sweet chocolate, grated
1 tablespoon butter
½ teaspoon vanilla
1 baked 9-inch pie shell
4 ounces Mija candy or finely crushed Almond Roca candy

DIRECTIONS
Combine sugar, cornstarch, and salt. Add ¼ cup of milk, mixing well. Blend in egg yolks and set aside. Dissolve cocoa in ¼ cup of milk. Mix in grated chocolate and set aside. Scald 1½ cups of milk in saucepan over moderate heat. Whisk in cornstarch mixture until smooth. Continue to cook, whisking, until clear and thickened. Whisk in the cocoa mixture. Cook, whisking, until chocolate melts and mixture is thick. Remove from heat. Add butter and vanilla. Stir until butter melts. Refrigerate until thoroughly chilled. Turn into baked pie shell. Sprinkle Mija Toffee Candy over top (see following recipe). Refrigerate until chilled. Serves 10 to 12.

Mija Toffee Candy

1 cup sugar
1 cup butter (not margarine)
3 ounces slivered almonds
1 tablespoon water
1 tablespoon white corn syrup
1 four-ounce bar Hershey's chocolate

DIRECTIONS:
Combine sugar, butter, almonds, water, and syrup in a heavy saucepan. Cook and stir over high heat until amber colored. (It will smoke some, and almonds will look toasted.) Pour into buttered 9x13 inch pan. Spread evenly. Melt chocolate and gently spread over toffee. Cool. Crush or grind up for topping for Mija Pie.

John Elitch, a celebrated cook of the 1880s, is known for his beer garden turned amusement park. Unlike James Cole, Elitch was remembered for his skills at the stove long after the management of Elitch Gardens had relieved him of kitchen duties. Elitch cooked at the Arcade Restaurant at 1613 Larimer, whose fame was overshadowed by its gambling hall. Reporter Chet Letts mused that the Arcade was "once the center of all there was in Denver that glittered after evening milking time; when men won and were so happy that they drank themselves to death elbow to elbow with…others…drowning their sorrows." After the Arcade closed in 1918, Letts fondly remembered that it was a little more expensive than most restaurants in Denver, but the portions were generous and the food was better: "Elitch was the best chef in Denver, and [travelers] went out of their way to come and eat of his cooking. It was not known just what he did to a T-bone or a tenderloin, but he could serve a steak that men talked about in London and Hongkong."[29]

The Arcade was remodeled in 1891. Upon reopening, it was a "perfect gem of a room" and "as bright as one of Uncle Sam's silver dollars." There was attractive tiling, fashionable mahogany tables, and clean white linen. Every piece of china bore the restaurant's name. The mirrors around the room reflected light from large chandeliers powered by gas and electricity. Patrons found "oysters, game, and fish at all seasons of the year, delicacies of all kinds and cookery to please the most fastidious." Division of the icebox into "apartments" meant that the appliance could hold three thousand pounds of ice.[30]

THE MENU SPEAKS

The oldest Denver menu lives a quiet retirement in the Denver Public Library. The Colorado Pioneer Club, whose members arrived before 1861, held its 1882 annual dinner at Charpiot's Hotel Restaurant. This very special menu is only a snapshot of 1880s haute cuisine in Denver. The meal started with raw oysters, then Baltimore-style oyster soup, followed by fillet of trout *à la tartare* and then entrées of larded quail with escalloped oysters or roasted turkey stuffed with oysters. Dessert featured ice cream, Charlotte Russe, and several varieties of cake.

Aside from this one glorious menu, nineteenth-century restaurants' specialties are largely unknown. Hotel Toscano at 1535 Wewatta Street catered to the local Italian trade and advertised its skill in "risotto alla Milanese."[31] A 1902 newspaper report suggests that Condon's Café,

A menu from 1880s Denver is the rarest of artifacts. A printed bill of fare only made an appearance at special events like the 1882 banquet for of Colorado pioneers. *From Menu Collection, WH1509, Western History Collection, Denver Public Library.*

at 17th and Welton Streets, had a "good steak or a well-cooked English mutton chop…[a] specialty is Welsh rarebit and old ale, a tidbit well worth trying."[32] Menus appeared for special affairs, but restaurants posted everyday fare on chalkboards well past 1910 or hung hand-lettered posters high enough for everyone to see. Menus became the fashion after 1930, with improvements in transportation, refrigeration, preservation, and food processing technologies.

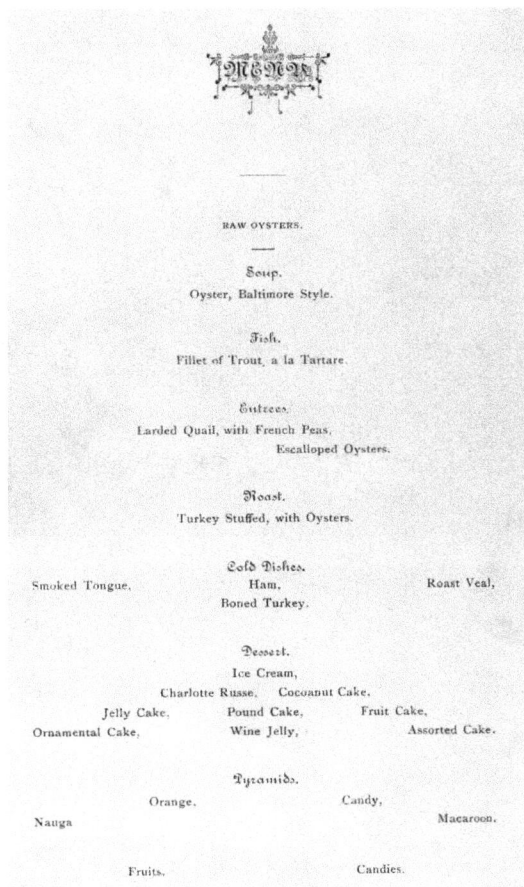

We take for granted that our favorite grocery store will have fresh apples in February because of international, refrigerated shipping from the southern hemisphere, where apples are ripening. However, in 1867, train service only came as far west as Julesburg, and the remaining 190 miles *could* be covered in thirty hours by stagecoach.[33] Throughout the nineteenth century, Denver restaurant ads used phrases like "all the delicacies of the season," "the best that the market affords," or "every delicacy of the season constantly subject to order." We know that the International Restaurant's 1860s menu included authentic French food and "choicest Delicacies of the market." Italian immigrant Dario Catignani used a similar phrase in his 1891 advertisement in *La Patria*, an Italian-language newspaper: "Le primizie delle Stagioni si trovano sempre in questo Albergo" ("The first fruits of the seasons are always in this Hotel"). Today's restaurant lingo might render these phrases as "farm fresh" or "locally sourced." The trendy "seasonal" menus of modern America were the reality of nineteenth-century cooking.

YOU CAN WORK HERE BUT YOU CAN'T EAT HERE

Immigrants and minorities found business opportunities resulting from denial of service in white, native born–owned restaurants, hotels, and boarding houses. Denver's rich history includes African Americans, Japanese, Chinese, Greek, German, Italian, and Mexican immigrants running restaurants, hotels, resorts, and boarding houses at the end of the nineteenth and the beginning of the twentieth centuries. Most of these minority restaurateurs served "American food" (steaks, eggs, sandwiches) for Americans. Some capitalized on homesickness, like the Hotel Toscano advertisement "si raccomanda agli Italiani" ("recommended to all Italians"). Racism and poverty prevented recording many of their stories or photographing businesses. Additionally, many available records are suspect or lack details.

There has been little examination of Denver's nineteenth-century minority entrepreneurs and their struggles. Except for Mary Randolph and

Opposite, top: Before the Golden Arches, lunchrooms like the American kept Denver fed at noontime. *Accession #CHS-X3457, History Colorado, Denver, Colorado.*

Opposite, bottom: Capelli's Place was one of the city's earliest Italian American–owned restaurants. My Brother's Bar currently occupies this location. *From* La Patria, *December 14, 1891.*

Hotel D'Italia on 1545 Larimer offered both lodging and meals to homesick Italian American emigrants in the 1890s. *From* La Patria, *December 14, 1891.*

James Stiles, who ran boarding houses in 1871, it seems that Barney Ford and H.O. Wagner are the only African Americans running restaurants in Denver until about 1887. Between 1887 and 1916, more than thirty-six African American men and women owned restaurants or boarding houses that offered day board. The statistics produced by the U.S. Census Bureau, the Department of Labor, show that Denver's African Americans were a scant 4 percent of the population well into the twentieth century. In 1929, only seven restaurants appear in a list of one hundred African American–owned businesses in Denver.

In 1895, the Colorado state legislature passed a law that stated that all persons were entitled to the "full and equal enjoyment" of the state's inns, restaurants, eating houses, barbershops, and public conveyances. Those violating this law could face fines ranging from $50 to $500. One commentator early in the twentieth century noted, "Flagrant violations of this, however, exist in Denver."[34]

In the 1890s, Will O. Smith ran the Five Points Café. His wife, Hariatt, ran a rooming house upstairs. Concurrently, African Americans began to move into the surrounding neighborhood. *From Western History Collection, DPL-73838, Denver Public Library.*

Unfortunately, racism helped us identify these business people. Denver city directories list African Americans and their businesses as "colored" into the twentieth century. The United States census used "W" for white, "B" for black, and "Jap" for Japanese, as well as other labels. Because these designations were at the discretion of the directory recorder or census enumerator, perceived education level, regional accents, and skin tones meant that recorders listed some African American family members as white and some as black. The extent that African Americans were undercounted is unknown.

There is general documentation of African American waiters, soda jerks, porters, cooks, and dishwashers. They even faced discrimination in the kitchen. For example, in 1902, when Denver's waiters and cooks went on strike, an article in the *Rocky Mountain News* was uncertain what the African American Union was going to do. In the early years, black waiters and cooks were a separate local from their white counterparts.

Although most African American–owned restaurants appear for fewer than three years in the city directories, five lasted more than a decade. The available records are not clear regarding which are restaurants and which are boarding houses with day board (European plans). Annie Scott, Harriet Sides, and Anna Wilson exemplify this. Listed in the city directories under "Restaurants," the census records show Scott and Sides owning boarding houses. Both beat the odds and were in business for ten or more years. Even today, 25 percent of all restaurants will close within the first year, and only 25 percent will stay open for more than a decade.

Scott and Sides were born in slavery, widowed, had children, moved at least once taking their businesses with them, and finally settled in Five Points. The 1900 and 1910 federal censuses record Annie (Anna) Scott as a cook with boarders. From 1898 to 1911, city directories list her under "Restaurants" at 45 Starr in the Elyria neighborhood and, after 1903, at 4691 Franklin Street. We know nothing of menu or prices for room or board.

City directories list Mrs. Harriet (Hattie) Sides with a restaurant at 1221 20th Street from 1895 to 1899. In 1900, she moved the business to 1922 Lawrence and moved again in 1907 to 1936 Lawrence Street, taking over from one Anna Wilson, also African American. John and Harriet Sides came to Denver before 1880 and were among the first African American families to move into Five Points.

John Henry Lewis didn't like the wind on his parents' farm in Kansas, so in 1890, at age twenty-two, he walked to Pueblo. He found work as dishwasher for $1.50 per week, plus a bed in the restaurant's attic. He learned how to cook, run the business, and manage money. In 1906, Lewis came to Denver and opened up his own restaurant. When interviewed in 1940, Lewis's motto was "Good food, honesty, and hard work." He reported that in his twenty-five years in Five Points, "white and black ate at the same table without any friction." The interviewer added, "Proving beyond any question of doubt the utter fallacy and rot of race segregation in public eating places." We failed to find Lewis in any other source.[35]

Other groups—Japanese, Chinese, and Mexican immigrants—found homes north of downtown between 19th and 20th Streets on Lawrence to Larimer as African Americans left for Five Points. Harriet Sides's restaurant location at 1221 20th Street remained a restaurant with a series of different Japanese owners, including Guy Sasaki's Fuji Chop Suey, which served noodles and short orders beyond 1930.

The Chinese were considered the lowest on the race scale. The 1871 Denver directory lists Yua Yang and his laundry as "Heathen Chinee."[36] They attracted few non-countrymen to their restaurants for the first twenty-five years that they were in Denver. At the most, Denver's Chinese population was 1,100 men working on the railroads. By 1890, there were a handful of women and about 980 Chinese men, of which 300 were laundrymen and 50 were cooks, porters, or waiters. Records point to Chin Poo as the first Chinese restaurateur who tried to attract non-Chinese. The January 6, 1890 *Rocky Mountain News* reported that

Chin "fitted up a restaurant for the whites…a Chinese cook prepares anything in Season. Their opium rooms are also clean and well aired." Another forty years would pass before effective narcotic regulations.

Two years after Chin Poo's landmark restaurant, anti-Chinese legislation passed, and with increasing anti-Chinese sentiment, their number dropped to 589, of which 405 were laundry men and 8 kept restaurants. A scant 306 lived in Denver's Chinatown in 1900, and by 1940, 110 remained. Race riots may indicate otherwise, but Denver's non-Chinese eventually grew fond of Chinese food. Perhaps its exotic nature brought 3,000 non-Chinese to Denver's 1910 Chinese New Year celebration.[37]

THE NEW CENTURY DAWNS AND IS OPEN ALL HOURS

By the 1890s, Denver was no longer isolated from the economic fits and starts endured by the rest of the nation. The Panic of 1893 hit the city as hard as any flood or fire from three decades earlier. Unaware of the broader

Restaurant, brothel…and haunted? The Navarre has been most of these. In the 1880s, the ladies dined discreetly in this room. *From Western History Collection, F-21541, Denver Public Library.*

The End Has Come

for Denver's world-famed Manhattan restaurant at 1635 Larimer street. It will close its doors at 7 a. m. Monday after forty-five years of uninterrupted, twenty-four-hours-a-day service. When the restaurant was founded by the late Richard Pinhorn, he hired Chris Rapp as night chef. Rapp, still on the job, still working the night shift, will be there to prepare the last meal. He is shown here.

◇　◇　◇　◇　◇

FAMED DENVER CAFE WILL CLOSE DOORS

Chef Chris Rapp broiled the steaks from The Manhattan's opening day in 1896 until the last meal in the early hours of April 21, 1941. *From the* Denver Post, *April 20, 1941, Western History Collection, Denver Public Library.*

economic uncertainty of this bleak era, the Works Progress Administration recalled in the 1940s, "It is reported that Denver in 1890 served the cheapest meals for the food put out in the United States. Steak, French-fried potatoes, bread and butter, coffee, and a desert, usually pie or bread pudding, was 15 cents. San Francisco came next with good meals for 20 cents."[38]

During the last decade of the old century, the restaurant that would be synonymous with Denver over the next four decades opened. The Manhattan at 1635 Larimer Street was the brainchild of English immigrant Richard Pinhorn. Pinhorn found his way to Denver in 1892, and within four years, he had created a restaurant about which the *Rocky Mountain News* recalled, "There was no fancy French cookery with spices and wines." Opening night saw Chris Rapp's first shift as night chef. Most likely, the German immigrant broiled his first of many thousands of steaks. Rapp was still at his post forty-five years later as he cooked The Manhattan's last meal. Cattle barons, the occasional member of royalty, and those with just enough money for a sandwich all found their way to The Manhattan. In the years after the Panic, Denver native Ruth Bradford recalled how her mother waited on an impoverished Baby Doe Tabor. Although her Matchless Mine had tapped out, Tabor dined at The Manhattan when visiting her brother, Peter McCourt, who roomed at the Windsor Hotel. Before or after those visits, Bradford's mother always served Baby Doe a roll and coffee. Colorado's first tragic heroine always left a nickel tip.[39]

Initiated by the venerable Baur's Restaurant style, The Manhattan, The Edelweiss Café, and Pell's Oyster House would define Denver dining in the new century. Restaurants like Baur's and Pell's specialized, while The Manhattan and The Edelweiss Café menus were comprehensive.

CHAPTER 2
The Regular Places and Madre and Otosan Find Homes

Adolescent Denver was considering the face that it would show to the world as the twentieth century dawned. The Panic of 1893 laid the town low, but the first post-pioneer generation of residents began to realize that tourism, transportation, and other non-mining economies could push the city toward a higher level of sophistication and some measure of respect as a member of the nation's leading metropolises.

During the next forty years, Denver would go through additional economic ups and downs. The next fiscal calamity—the Great Depression of the 1930s—saw people watching their pennies. Going out to eat was a rare treat, not an everyday occurrence. Growing up in north Denver during the 1930s, Carl Cerveny recalled that his family "only ate out once every couple of months. Usually, The Edelweiss or the Blue Parrot."[40]

Regardless of economic ups and downs, the number of dining places grew by the year. It was also a time of tourists, those stricken with tuberculosis, and others looking to start again finding themselves at the foot of the Rockies. In 1900, there were about 150 restaurants across Denver, and those were mostly between Larimer and Curtis Streets. By the Second World War, that number had leapt to 685. During those four decades, there were four stalwarts where a good meal was more or less guaranteed. Each was notable for the personalities of its owners as much as its food.

Baur's. The Manhattan. The Edelweiss Café. Pell's Oyster House. Each establishment in its own ads, and as well as newspaper articles, made the claim that it was either one of the great tourist attractions of the American

BLUE PARROT INN

DENVER
1718 BROADWAY
•

Dining Places of Distinction

IN HOLLYWOOD
GOURMET HOLLYWOOD

IN CHICAGO
LE PETIT GOURMET

IN OAK PARK
BLUE PARROT PATIO

Minnie the Parrot was a regular at Denver's Blue Parrot Inn during the 1930s and 1940s. *From authors' collection.*

West or the greatest place to eat between the Atlantic and Pacific. There were other notable survivors—the five McVittie's located across the city, Tortoni's at 1541–47 Arapahoe, George Watrous Restaurant at 1525 Curtis, and the

Blue Parrot at 1716–30 Broadway. The majority of the dining stories mainly come back to the Big Four. At least two of the four (The Manhattan and The Edelweiss Café) boasted wide-ranging menus constructed to offer whatever the customer wanted at whatever time of the day. The little guy, and gal, who served the city's diners began the century with a desire to get a little bit more.

OYSTERS ON THE ROCKIES

One of the first of Denver's celebrity restaurateurs, George W. Pell Sr., came from Brooklyn to Denver in 1881. Pell brought to the Rockies a Brooklynite's knowledge of oysters and his own rules for running an establishment. Pell promised to "Bring the Sea Shore to Denver Every Day," but the city soon knew that he was not above closing his Oyster House during the summer and tossing out those who lit up cigarettes or cigars after a meal. He followed the old adage not to eat oysters in months without the letter *r*—May, June, July, and August. The middle of the year is also the time of fertility for oysters, as well as the hottest and most difficult time to ship fresh seafood.

Over a five-decade run, Pell's Oyster House had two locations before settling at the alley between Glenarm Place and Welton Street for its last sixteen years. Pell's menu caused even hardened newspaper reporters to go all

PELL'S

Denver's Famous
Fish and
Oyster House

▫ ▫ ▫

1514-18 WELTON STREET

▫ ▫ ▫

We Bring the
Sea Shore to Denver
Every Day

▫ ▫ ▫

RETAIL DEPT.   MAIN 378

George Pell brought the ocean to Denver in the 1880s. His Oyster House defied topography until the 1930s. *From Western History Collection, Denver Public Library.*

Following the old ways, Pell kept his Denver fish house at 520–524 16th Street closed in months containing the letter *r*. *From Western History Collection, X-29479, Denver Public Library.*

poetic. The *Denver Republican* noted, "Located near the center of the continent, he reaches out with equal facility to all points of the compass and draws his table supplies from the Atlantic, the Pacific, the northern lakes and the inland streams and furnishes his patrons with the finest, freshest oysters, fresh and salt water fish, lobsters, crabs, clams and all popular sea foods." Pell employed seventeen people, and his house sat forty-eight. Pell died on Christmas Eve 1911. His wife and his son, George, continued to run the place. After their deaths, others owned Pell's before it was finally closed in 1937, partially a victim of the overharvesting and pollution of the oyster beds of New York.[41]

MEMORY IS SELECTIVE

The Manhattan entered the new century as the undisputed people's restaurant. With a choice of offerings better suited for a library than a menu,

Richard Pinhorn's Manhattan kept serving the charcoal-broiled sirloins, a combination salad, French-fried onions, and potatoes around the clock every day. This meal combination was imitated by hundreds of restaurants across the city over the rest of the century. One signature item was the onion rings.

Use Bermuda Onions. Slice into circles or rings and drop in whipping cream first. Then dip the rings in salted flour and covering them completely. Drop them again in whipping cream and again in salted flour. Drop them in boiling grease and allow them to cook for about seven minutes.[42]

According to Pinhorn, hanging the steaks and aging them until they were blue was the secret to a meal that brought customers back. Pinhorn was a walking embodiment of civic pride. At the close of the First World War, he was lauded for keeping his restaurant's prices down despite wartime profiteering. It was said that he fed the hungry if they came looking for a handout. When Pinhorn died in 1922, his will listed eleven charities for bequests. Residents took up a collection two years later and erected a granite and bronze sidewalk memorial.

Unfortunately, there is a quiet and forgotten pall over the upbeat story of Denver's

The memorial to Richard Pinhorn first stood in front of The Manhattan at 1551 Larimer. Since the early 1970s, it has welcomed visitors to the 1400 block of Larimer. *Photo by Kristen Autobee.*

45

Manhattan. Sometime during the first week of March 1903, an African American entered The Manhattan in the company of a white man and woman. A fight ensued, and a chef came out with a rolling pin in his hand from the kitchen. The cook's aim was off the mark, and he struck a waiter by mistake. The *Denver Times* newspaper reported that the African American escaped the trouble uninjured.[43]

The mêlée resulted in manager Charles Harding drawing a "color line," with the announcement that "no negroes shall be served with meals there."[44] Sadly, the ban remained in place until they closed the business thirty-eight years later. The Manhattan clearly had a pecking order for minority groups. As an advertiser in the *Denver Jewish News* during the early 1920s, the restaurant clearly stated, "Jewish Trade Solicited."[45]

The Manhattan's farewell after forty-some years on April 21, 1941, was the opportunity for both Denver dailies to serve up a large portion of lament with a dollop of hyperbole. The *Denver Post* noted that "a nationally-known link between the Denver of yesterday and the Denver of today will be broken," that the Larimer establishment "ranked among the most important tourist attractions of the west," and, finally, that "[t]he claim a few years ago that the Manhattan had served more charcoal broiled steaks than any other restaurant in the world was never disputed."[46]

That same week, Denver's African American newspaper, the *Colorado Statesman*, took the high road when noting The Manhattan's passing:

> *The Famous Manhattan restaurant has folded up, closed its doors, as Time has whispered: "You have served during a given period." Unhappily, Negroes cannot share the many memories enjoyed by others who have frequented this legendary establishment, wherefore its closing, along with other crumblings, means only the opening of new doors, to new philosophies, where the Manhattan would not fit, so peace be to its ashes.[47]*

The Manhattan's legacy survived Larimer's descent into skid row. After closing in the 1940s, The Manhattan went from steaks and onion rings to shots and beers as the Ginn Mill. In the late 1950s, Pinhorn's nephew felt that the bronze cherub in front of the Ginn Mill had seen too much and asked for its relocation. After a long search, a group of Larimer Street businesses resettled the statue in a Larimer Square walkway in 1971, where it remains today.

THOSE WHO SERVE

Labor versus management was a slow, simmering cauldron in Denver as early as the 1890s. Add hatred toward Japanese emigrants, and the entire atmosphere was a poisonous stew. In July 1901, the Cooks' Union picketed and urged a boycott of three Japanese-owned restaurants on Larimer Street. Japanese immigrant George O'Hara employed Japanese cooks and non-union white waiters at two of the restaurants. The union insisted that the waiters join. O'Hara responded that if the white waiters joined, so should the Japanese cooks.

But the constitutions of the Waiters' and Cooks' Unions clearly stated that "all members must be American citizens," and it was well understood that these organizations were for whites only. So, the union refused the Japanese cooks membership, and O'Hara refused to hire union waiters. Soon, pickets warned passersby to guard "against possible non-union indigestion." O'Hara fought back and contacted the Japanese ambassador in Washington, D.C. The Japanese consul in San Francisco wrote to Denver's mayor demanding protection for Japanese citizens. The union eventually defused the situation after it promised a federal court judge to abstain from boycotting and picketing the restaurants.[48]

In addition to labor and race, the cleanliness of the city's restaurants was another concern. A 1902 *Denver Times* columnist wrote with a mixture of civic pride and nausea: "Nowhere else do you find such good, wholesome food, to begin with; cooking that is so uniformly good; such fresh butter, real cream, good milk, good beef, and coffee that is clear, strong and the genuine article. But there is a serious drawback to some of the smaller places and that is the too lavish display of—sticky flypaper!"[49]

Waitresses' hours were long, and pay was meager. At the start of the twentieth century, a male, Euro-American waiter could make ten to twenty dollars per week. Some places prohibited "fees" or tipping, but a waiter at Tortoni's admitted to making two to four dollars a day for good service. For a few days in 1902, a few waitresses were not going to take it anymore. Some of the city's waitresses had enough of making eight dollars a week.[50]

A *Denver Republican* account captured the moment at 6:30 p.m. on a Saturday when August Schaibly's staff at the Admiral (1629 Champa Street) walked off the dining room floor. After serving the entrée course, five waitresses "advanced threateningly" on Schaibly, asking for ten dollars per week. He countered with eight dollars per week and board. At that moment, "With one exulting, joyous pull the knots on five aprons were untied and five aprons came off. Ten hands reached for two raglans, three jackets and five hats, and five waitresses joined the passing throng on Champa Street, while Mr. Schaibly tried to distribute food among the waiting patrons of the restaurant."[51]

Schaibly offered a condescending promise that it would "take a week" to learn how to be a waitress, but it took a lifetime to be a good cook. The waitresses picketed the Admiral and asked others to boycott the restaurant until their demands were met. The women were not successful. Later that year, a ballot referendum passed establishing an eight-hour workday in Colorado. However, the state legislature refused to implement the will of the people until the following year.

"Every Man Is His Own Waiter"

Management and labor tensions had spread from the state's mines and rail yards to the streets of Denver by spring 1903. What began in March as a protest against two teamsters joining a union soon spread into sympathy strikes. In May, more than six hundred waiters and cooks joined Denver's butchers, brewery workers, and trades people on the picket line. Many of Denver's restaurants closed or, like the owners of The Manhattan, encouraged "self-service" among their patrons. At the Palace Bakery, one special customer's hunger temporarily arrested labor's action:

> Policeman Baldwin was the only person who ate breakfast in the Palace bakery and lunch room on Fifteenth street near Lawrence after the order to strike was issued. The place was crowded when the waitresses stopped work suddenly and began taking off their apron[s]...A large juicy pork chop had just been placed before Baldwin and he purposed to eat it. Reaching down in his hip pocket, he pulled out his .45, placed across his lap and then went on calmly eating his breakfast. "This may be the last square meal I'll get for a month," remarked the policeman, "and I'm going to eat it or there'll be something doing."[52]

An anti-union organization, the Denver Citizens Alliance, with ties to management and Colorado Republican governor James Peabody, faced off against an amalgam of workers' groups led by the American Labor Union (ALU). As May wore on, the Denver dailies went from lighthearted stories of bankers packing their own lunches to towering headlines warning of an impending general strike. After days of negotiations, on May 21, both the Citizens Alliance and the ALU agreed to recognize the right of workers to join the ALU and to rehire employees. Denver's employers soon violated the agreement and blacklisted those workers who participated in the sympathy strike.[53]

THE BAKERY AND THE *BOITE*

If you were a late-night theatergoer on Curtis Street during the twentieth century's early days (and nights), you would eventually find your way to The Edelweiss Café and Bakery at 1649 California.

Operated by Charles Suchotzki for many years, The Edelweiss had reached the status of "local dining institution" by the 1930s. Staying open until 3:00 a.m. during the weekdays, it drew Curtis Street vaudevillians, newspapermen, cops, and horse players. From an overhead balcony came music from an Ampico Grand Player Piano. Denver's hoi polloi sat under one roof to enjoy their "Club" sixty-cent dinner. A Club dinner could include anything from "one-half milk-fed chicken" to "grilled pounded rump steak

The Edelweiss served Denver's lunch and after-theater crowds at 16th and California for most of the early twentieth century. *From authors' collection.*

au natural," with vegetables, dessert, and a beverage. The Edelweiss baked its own pastries and served cheesecake. More than two decades after its closure, newspaperman Sam Lusky recalled a typical night at the Edelweiss. "A jolly fat waitress named Opal would serve you a scrumptious hamburger for just 25 cents and was always in such good spirits she lifted you out of whatever doldrums into which you might have slipped." During the 1950s, a diner could have either boiled ham hocks or fried fillet of lemon sole for the same price: ninety-five cents.[54]

Baur's Survives

Baur's benefitted from the popularity of soda fountains and confectioners from the late nineteenth century until Colorado's 1915 prohibition. During the 1910s, Baur's advertised regularly in the *Colorado Statesman*, Denver's primary African American newspaper. The family defied protests and served the racially mixed party of contralto Marian Anderson when she performed in Denver a few decades later.[55]

Baur's menu was filled with the old standards that Denver liked—potted Swiss steak with brown gravy, fresh mountain trout sauté with choice of vegetable and potato balls, and grilled liberty steak (also known as hamburger). Federal price controls instituted under the Emergency Price Control Act of 1946 ensured that the average price for a complete dinner ranged from $0.85 to $1.70. But times and tastes changed. In her article on Baur's history, "Sweet Magic: One Hundred Years of Baur's Restaurant," Lee Jacobs Carlin wrote, "By the 1960s, the cost of serving quality flavors based on the finest butter, cream, and chocolate could not compete with the onslaught of the scientifically engineered franchise."[56]

Urban renewal had no room for tradition, no matter how sweet, and in 1970, Baur's closed two years short of a century. Baur's departure more than forty years ago left a cavity for Denver's sweet tooth that is only now being filled by a renaissance of small, imaginative bakeries and confectioners.

Denver boasted a lively theater and vaudeville scene until the arrival of movies and the radio. A handful of places to eat within walking distance from the city's Theater Row on Curtis Street served actors, chorus girls, cops, and others who earned a coin after dark. One of these haunts was McVittie's. Owners Albert and Bonnie McVittie ran an establishment known for its after-dark characters, contrasting with the décor's gleaming white tile floors

Baur's had expanded out of downtown by the mid-1950s to the new Cherry Creek Shopping Center. The building now houses Elway's. *From authors' collection.*

McVittie's was on nearly every Denver block in the 1920s. The thought of being the forty-ninth person to occupy one of the counter stools remains disconcerting. *From Western History Collection, F-37934, Denver Public Library.*

and walls. McVittie's newspaper publicity claimed that every day, forty-nine poeple sat in each chair of its restaurants. Ruth Bradford recalled that often behind the picture window of these McVittie's was someone dressed like a "mammy" flipping pancakes.[57]

The Mozart at 1647 Curtis was the best-known "after-theater" spot in the early days of the twentieth century. The Mozart featured a front bar with a free lunch counter and a small room with booths in the back of the building. For the cost of a nickel beer, you could have sliced cheeses, meat, pickles, olives, French fries, or bread. The Mozart served a whole roast pig complete with apple and a roast turkey on Christmas and New Year's Day.[58]

By the time of the Great War in Europe, and as the scourge of Spanish influenza crossed the planet, city officials had become concerned about the spread of disease. As citizens were encouraged to plant "war gardens" in the city's vacant lots and alleys, the municipal administration became increasingly aware of cleanliness in public places like hospitals, hotels, barbershops, and restaurants. In June 1918, the city's health inspection department awarded certificates for cleanliness and sanitary conditions to sixteen restaurants. These included well-known and heavily patronized restaurants like The Manhattan and Pell's as well as places lost to time like the J. Zimmerlie Lunch Room at 1625 Stout. The remaining 275 Denver restaurants were left with a blank space on the wall where the health department certificate might have hung.[59]

Denver's "name" restaurants dominated the local dining scene until the end of the 1940s. Almost forgotten were the places where the city's working class and ethnic groups ate their meals. One can discern a great deal of Denver's character from the different kinds of restaurants there—from ladies' tea to a bowl of chili at lunch to an adventure in the bazaar of ethnic restaurants found in storefronts.

LADIES WHO LUNCH

Ladies were the primary market of the city's tearooms. As the day wore on, women of the post-Victorian era had other needs. However, Denver's police and fire boards were there to stop them. In April 1909, these boards issued an order forbidding women unaccompanied by escort to enter restaurants serving liquor after 8:00 p.m. The boards were certain "only in rare instances that a respectable woman" would want to drink on her own at that hour. The city's clubwomen took exception and found the order to be "a discrimination against the freedom of the women of Denver." The boards justified their decision "to clean the streets and also the restaurants and rooming houses of women of questionable character and those drastic measures had been found necessary to accomplish this object."[60] Three years later, the boards modified a ban on vocal music that allowed singing as long as the songs were "not of the suggestive kind." They hired a censor to ensure that singers avoided using that summer's scandalous hit "Oh! You Kid!" in their nightly repertoire. Police, lacking a sense of rhythm, shut down any café where vulgar songs were on the musical bill of fare.[61]

The city's constabulary was only taking orders from the city's fathers to purge Denver of any remaining traces of its Wild West beginnings. Meanwhile, other groups helping to build the city were living their lives in an unfamiliar atmosphere, often with only the comfort of food to remind them of home.

Hell-Fire Stew

Like in other American cities in the new century, chili (or "chile," the preferred spelling during the early twentieth century) parlors or "joints" kept the working poor from starving to death. Larimer between 17th and 28th Streets held most of Denver's chili joints. A 1902 *Denver Times* article noted, "They are crowded during the day, but the most business is done at night, when the places are thronged with people of all classes and colors." Mexican nationals weren't the ethnic group to introduce, or own, these joints to Denver. Unfortunately, some owners were not shy about identifying their desired client base. The White Peoples Chile Parlor was not in downtown Birmingham, Alabama, or on the outskirts of Jackson, Mississippi, but at 1727 Curtis in Denver during the 1910s. Other Denver chili parlors avoided a big bowl of hate with the spice of ethnicity. C.K. Pappas and M. Karavites owned the Old Mexico Chile & Coffee House from 1907 into the 1940s. The two Greeks boasted, "We make Chile our own way."[62]

Upon entering the average Denver chili joint, brave souls found a long counter and high stools. The meals were served at the counter and prepared behind a partition or separate kitchen away from the prying eyes of the prospective diner. Men, women, and children sat at the counter together and ate with tin spoons. One price for all: five cents. The higher-class chili parlor made room for tables, while others provided private dining booths for the ladies.[63]

How to describe this spicy gruel for the masses? Once again, the *Times* noted:

> It is a kind of soup, made from beef, beans and chile peppers. The beef is cut into small squares and boiled into a broth: the beans are of the brown Mexican kind and are cooked separately and added when the broth is done. Chile enough to make it smart and burn is cooked in the

Colorado had an anti-discrimination law in public places by the 1890s, but that didn't stop the owner of White Peoples Chile Parlor (center) from displaying his prejudices to all of Denver. *From Western History Collection, MCC-4056, Denver Public Library.*

> *broth. The whole is of reddish-brown color and hot enough to make the uninitiated cry for water.*

The *Times* correspondent found in one parlor a new dish for a new century: liverling. Liver, white beans, onions, and potatoes were ground to pulp and cooked in water until served. The consistency of apple butter, liverling as a dining phenomenon did not last long enough to qualify as the city's first dining specialty.[64]

Only few blocks apart, the chili parlor and the department store tearoom existed in separate hemispheres. Nearly forgotten in this age of national chains like Macy's and Dillard's is that department stores in mid-century America were sources of civic pride. In Pittsburgh, it was Horne's; in Cincinnati, Pogues; and in St. Louis, Stix, Baer & Fuller. In Denver, it was the Denver Dry Goods—later just "the Denver." Its tearoom on the sixth floor of its flagship store at 16th and California was established early in the twentieth century. As late as the 1960s, the Denver Dry Goods tearoom was serving about three thousand lunches per

The Great Depression was only a few months away, but this group of former Union Pacific railroad employees gazes solemnly before dinner at the Denver Dry Goods tearoom. *From authors' collection.*

day. Nancy Brueggeman, wife of a Denver Dry Goods executive vice-president, often lunched at their tearoom. Even in 1969, Brueggeman described the setting as "white tablecloths, lovely ambience." She recalled eating with her husband in a special section just for staff but also with the children in the main dining area. Brueggeman related that even women who would not or could not buy dresses at the Denver would not eat lunch at any other store's tearoom. In those days, the quality of the tearoom's food brought as many people to the Denver as the annual January White Sale.[65]

The Denver Dry Goods tearoom had the following standard on its menu for a number of years:

Chicken à la King

2 sticks butter	1½ cups flour
8 cups chicken stock or more (canned broth may be used)	1 cup half and half
1 pound cooked, skinned chicken meat, diced	1 large red bell pepper, cut in ¼-inch strips
1 large green bell pepper, cut in ¼-inch strips	½ pound sliced mushrooms, sautéed in butter
salt and white pepper to taste	baked puff pastry shells

Melt butter in large saucepan. Whisk in flour, cooking over moderate heat a few minutes. Still whisking, gradually add chicken stock. Cook over moderate heat, whisking until thickened. Whisk in half and half. Cook over low heat about 25 minutes. Add more chicken stock depending on desired consistency. Add remaining ingredients. Cook over low heat about 20 minutes. Serve in pastry shells. Serves 8.[66]

The Denver Dry Goods did not corner the market on light lunches. As the century wore on, local department stores like May D&F and Neusteter's Department Store had tearooms where two generations of women who found empowerment through shopping took their breaks. May D&F featured the Leadville Room in its University Hills outpost and the Lookout Room in the Westland Shopping Center on West Colfax Avenue in Lakewood. Neusteter's tearoom in Cherry Creek was called The Penthouse. Like automats and cafeterias, the tearoom is barely a memory of where women had light lunch. Brueggeman noted that tearooms were "a point of pride for a department store." Light lunches are still with us, but it is impossible to enjoy one in a downtown department store.

Daniels & Fisher menu. *Papers of Pierre Wolfe, WH1465, Western History Collection, Denver Public Library.*

Denver's Own *Comida*

In the early twenty-first century, it seems that every metro area block has at least one Mexican restaurant. Over the past one hundred years, Denver has seen countless Mexican restaurants come, go, and contribute dishes unique to the convergence of Mexico and the United States. Many mysteries surround the origins of Denver's contributions to Mexican American food culture.

A 1922 Denver business directory offers a tantalizing glimpse into the *raíces* (roots)—and future—of Denver dining. In the waning days of the Mexican Revolution, Modesto Disguez owned Mexico Libre (Free Mexico) at 2123 Larimer Street. There is little documentation on Disguez as owner. History unfairly has left few clues to claim this as the city's first true Mexican restaurant owned by someone of Mexican descent.[67]

The earliest description of a Denver restaurant owned by Mexican nationals or Mexican Americans comes from a curious *gringo* by the name of David Raffelock. Writing in a long-forgotten but intriguing arts magazine, *The Echo*, Raffelock ventured into El Nuevo Chapultepec somewhere on Larimer in the late fall of 1925:

> *We enter and are greeted with curious, cool glances…Mexicans sit eating food, tearing off huge pieces of enchiladas, talking in their native tongue. Senorita, behind the counter, looks shyly at us…We order chile of the comely senorita and were served by the heavy-set, swarthy man of the place. Hot, peppery chile it was, thick rich soup and many beans. For this sufficing meal we paid ten cents each…Like so many foreign restaurants, this one is more than a mere eating place. Mexican housewives come here for food not to be purchased in the ordinary American store. Workingmen come for the spiced, peppered foods to which they are accustomed.*[68]

The 1920s business directories do not list El Nuevo Chapultepec. The only clue Raffelock provided was a neighborhood along Larimer displaying "the faded riotous glory of bordellos" that by the age of the flapper had become "only a slum street now; seen from a Mexican restaurant where English is rarely spoken."[69]

The tastes and sensations that Americans love about this country's adaptations of Mexican food would only gather steam—and travel outside traditional Mexican neighborhoods—over the next two decades. Denver's newspapers played it safe when it came to introducing new tastes to their

Special Christmas and New Year's Dinners

Deliciously prepared as Meals always are at

The Broadway Rotisserie Inn

French and Italian Restaurant

Major Avondale, Mgr. and Owner

Booths-Tables   1748 Broadway

From time to time advertisers in THE ECHO are written up by Peggy. Turn to her page in this issue and read her breezy, helpful comments.

In the early twentieth century, French and Italian dishes lived hospitably on the same menu in many Denver restaurants, including at the Broadway Rotisserie Inn. *From Menu Collection, WH1509, Western History Collection, Denver Public Library.*

readers. A feature in the August 1, 1943 *Rocky Mountain News* lauded Mrs. Gertrude Reed, the owner of Casa Rosa de Oro, for "glibly" pronouncing "tortillas, tacos, Jamaica, bunello, and dozens of other names of Mexican dishes." Despite her glib use of Spanish, Mrs. Reed was completely straight-faced about the reasons why she launched a Mexican restaurant. "One day I was playing a game of bridge with a group of friends and we were discussing the lack of restaurants with atmosphere in Denver and right then I decided never to play at another bridge table until I had done something to remedy this."[70]

Reed was able to find "a helper," Manuel Trujillo. "We don't use recipes," Reed explained. "Because Manuel and I understand one another, when we say a pinch of salt or three fingers of sugar, or milk up to here in the blue casserole and so far we haven't had any failures."[71]

While society ladies went slumming in front of a stove of frijoles and green chili, other ethnicities were pleasing their communities and enticing the occasional outsider.

THE BIG STEW

Denver's Italian immigrants had been part of the city's life since the gold rush. A handful soon operated hotels, restaurants, meat markets, and bakeries. The Italian American enclave northwest of downtown had begun to take on its own character by the late nineteenth century. A number of early Denver restaurants served Italian as part of a menu dominated by French cuisine. One of the earliest places to stand on its own was Occioni's at 2454 19th Street. The menu boasted of veal piccata. Occioni's advertised that it was free of the element of danger that most Anglo-Americans associated with Italians. At least that's what *The Echo* magazine advised to Denver's limited number of bohemians during the 1920s: "Sr. Occioni serves nothing but the very best of food, and his patrons are free from disagreeable disturbances of any kind."[72]

Denver's Jewish community ate and socialized in delicatessens and lunch rooms mostly located between 16th and 18th, and Larimer and Curtis, as well as along West Colfax between downtown and Sheridan Boulevard. *Echo* magazine's ambassador to the city's many cuisines and cultures, David Raffelock, described a kosher restaurant just off Larimer Street. This was possibly Sam Brody's New York Kosher Delicatessen and Lunch Room at 1652 Larimer, or maybe Mrs. Rosen's Lunch Room at 1731 Curtis, or Bergman's at 922 18th Street—Raffelock did not specify. Men chatted in Yiddish with the hostess and enjoyed "soup with kasha, borsht…chopped liver with onions…Strictly kosher, too. With a regular meal, no butter was served. Plates piled high with well-baked white bread and rye."[73]

An observer from the Works Progress Administration found in the 1940s that Greek immigrants in Denver "catered to the sweet tooth of the American

Occioni's was a downtown outpost, as many Italian immigrants and second-generation Americans resided in north Denver. *From* The Echo, *Denver Public Library, Western History Collection.*

The bill of fare at a long-forgotten Greek restaurant in Denver. The menu items are Greek, but the prices seem fair. *From* The Echo, *Denver Public Library, Western History Collection.*

people…The most widespread and successful Greek business ventures are confectionery and fruit stores to which in Denver, the restaurant has been added. One needs only to stroll through downtown Denver to observe this."[74]

Denver's African American population was expanding to the small bungalows and clapboard houses north of Larimer and Lawrence Streets during the first half of the twentieth century. In 1920, the city of Denver's population totaled 256,941. Of that number, 6,075 were African American. According to the 1940 census, Denver had grown to 322,412, while the number of African Americans had slowly increased to 7,836. Surprisingly, over the three census reports from 1920 to 1940, Denver counted more African Americans than San Francisco, Portland, and Seattle. For the 1920 and 1930 pollings, it topped Oakland, California.[75]

The response to the reality of daily racism for Denver's African Americans was for the community to form its own clubs and resorts. These organizations provided social affairs, services, and meals. William A. Rice was a "soda dispenser" at Shaw's Drug Store in 1911. According to the *Colorado Statesman*, Rice opened a lunch buffet "equipped with all sanitary improvements, such as steam table, everything enclosed and all the cooking done before your eyes, no mistake to be made about its cleanliness. Mr. Rice is a hard worker in all lines for the advancement of his race and will be pleased to meet all his friends in and out of our city, 2014 Champa Street." Rice's buffet ownership was brief, as the Denver city directories for 1912 and 1913 have no listing for William A. Rice.[76]

Those restaurants that advertised in the *Statesman* in the 1910s indicate that the African American community did not stand alone and often mingled with other cultures' cuisines. In those days, the Oriental Restaurant at 1848 Arapahoe regularly advertised the all-American creation chop suey, noodles, and short orders to the *Statesman*'s readers. The real mix in the kitchen was the 5 Points Café at 2721 Welton, whose advertising lured customers with "Chop Suey, Noodles and All Kinds of Chinese Japanese and American Dishes. Short Orders at All Hours."[77] A contemporary observer wrote of the city's ethnic restaurants on Larimer to the north: "Thus is Denver's Greece, Italy, Jerusalem, Mexico and China—all with their coal stoves, uncovered tables, low prices and tipless waiters.[78]

The economic depression of the 1930s made life more difficult for the city's African Americans. Only one out of every four African Americans in Denver had a job in 1931. The establishments, located in and out of Five Points, which advertised in the city's only African American newspaper, underscore the reality that minority groups often bonded together economically when rejected by the dominant Euro-American culture. In 1940 Christmas ads, the neighborhood's main street was "Where Good Fellows Get Together" at the St. Louis Barbecue Inn at 2856 Welton, and Mae Chung's Yuye Café at 2801 Welton featured "Chinese Barbecue" with a special of "Home Cooked Pig's Feet" for five cents. They wished their customers a "happy holidays," as did other establishments on 28th Avenue, Larimer Street, and elsewhere across Five Points.[79]

The Second World War's aftermath affected these neighborhoods as Denver grew and suburbs sprouted in all directions. The dishes favored by African Americans remained bottled up in Five Points, as many Anglo-Americans leaned on racial stereotypes and missed trying something different and delicious.

Next, we will stop to pick up something quick and steeped in local flavor from two take-away icons: the Rockybilt hamburger and north Denver's canoli.

CHAPTER 3
An Order to Go

ROCKYBILTS, HORRIBLEBURGERS, AND THE ENIGMA OF NORTH DENVER'S CANOLI

Vegan or meathead, no one can ignore the all-encompassing significance of the hamburger in American life. Denver, like most American cities, had its own local spin on the people's steak. The Mile High City's contribution, the Rockybilt, reappears like Banquo's ghost on today's Denver menus despite having left the scene more than three decades ago. The Rockybilt hamburger has hung on, while other pillars of civic stability—Stapleton Airport, Mile High Stadium, and the *Rocky Mountain News*—eventually gave way and crumbled.

The city's Italian neighborhood made its own small contribution to fast food: the canoli. Or is it cannoli with two *n*'s? Or connolle? In a ten-block radius of the original Italian enclave, north Denver, the humble sausage roll answers to many names. Today's diners can still find the canoli at the takeout counter at Lechuga's at 3609 Tejon or fancier, sit-down places like Gaetano's at 38th and Navajo. Gaetano's Tasty Treat is the same as the canoli at Lechuga's: Italian sausage, provolone, and a green pepper strip wrapped and baked inside pizza dough.

Rockybilts and canolis reflect Denver's get-something-to-go, working-class side. Other cities may have deeper ethnic traditions and stronger class distinctions, but both dishes are like the people and the restaurants described in this book: not a lot of self-promotion and capable of working up a pretty good crave that occasionally needs satisfying.

CHEESEBURGER ON SPEER

Louis Ballast was the width of a slice of American cheese from becoming the originator of the cheeseburger. A monument on Speer Boulevard acknowledges his contribution. *Photo by Kristen Autobee.*

Before advertising agencies raised golden arches and haunted the public with creepy monarchs with oversized heads, every Denver neighborhood had its own stand or counter ready to sell you a hamburger.

Some hold close an urban myth that the world's first cheeseburger was created along Speer Boulevard during the 1930s. The legend says that in the mid-1930s, Louis Ballast operated the keg-shaped Humpty Dumpty Barrel Drive-In, soon known in the neighborhood as the "Barrel House." Looking for a gimmick, Ballast initially tried Hershey bars and peanut butter on top of a cooked beef patty. Perhaps more in tune with tastes of the early twenty-first century, the combination of meat and chocolate did not appeal to 1930s palates.

Undaunted, Ballast tried a slice of cheese on the patty, *et voilà*. Good idea it was, but Ballast's next move was even better. He filed an official Application and Affidavit for Registration of a Food Trademark, "cheeseburger," on March 5, 1935. Despite good intentions, Ballast never completed the application process. Ballast's son, David, deadpanned to the *Denver Post* in 2011, "That's why I'm not a millionaire."

A Pasadena lunch counter claims that it first served this concoction in 1924, and Kaelin's Restaurant in Louisville, Kentucky, keeps a 1934 menu as its holy shroud when making its claim to creating the first cheeseburger. The cheeseburger most likely existed before Ballast, but he made the marriage between meat, cheese, and a bun legal in Colorado.[80] The senior Ballast died in 1975, and a bank now occupies 2776 Speer Boulevard. A granite plinth in the bank's parking lot commemorates Ballast's Humpty Dumpty and his creation.

TAK-HOMA-SAK

Small ironies make great history. In 1921, Wichita resident Billy Ingram withdrew $700 from a local bank. The transaction founded an institution dedicated to serving small hamburgers that could be gobbled quickly and digested torturously: the White Castle. It didn't help that White Castle "steam-grilled" its burgers and was plagued by rumors of what kind of meat and the quality thereof lay hidden behind the castle walls.

Denver's Rockybilt chain advertised that you could "TAK-HOMA-SAK," but it still could serve its sliders on its own vitrified china. *Photo by Robert Autobee.*

White Castle never established a battlement along the Rockies, probably due to the efforts of Ingram's onetime Wichita neighbor, Roy Chesney. Elsewhere in the dry Southwest, another member of the Chesney family had opened a chain of short-order restaurants in Texas. Known as Rockefellers, Roy Chesney was aware of its success. Focused on Colorado, Chesney brought this idea west and, with a bit of tinkering, named his restaurant Rockybilt to honor the state's most recognizable feature, the Rockies.

The Rockybilt was a mile-high version of the White Castle with a crucially different special sauce surfing between patty and bun. At various times between the 1970s and 1990s, the *Rocky Mountain News* divulged the secret of this sauce, as follows.

Rockybilt Hamburger Sauce

Mix equal parts of:
light salad mustard
sweet pickle relish
Heinz 57 sauce

Variation: Mix 2 parts of yellow mustard, 1 part of tomato puree, and enough dill relish to suit taste and consistency.[81]

On a July day in 1969—the last day for Denver's first Rockybilt restaurant on East Colfax Avenue—Roy Chesney talked about his highlights over the previous thirty-three years. Chesney's memories began with opening day on July 17, 1936: "We opened for less than an hour the night before. We were working around getting to open and a couple of police officers came by so we fed them."[82]

In the summer of 1936, the Depression still had a tight grip in Denver. The state estimated that between 20 and 30 percent of Denver's households were "supported out of federal, state or local funds"[83] Hard times pushed the twenty-eight-year-old journalism graduate away from long hours in the newsroom toward long hours in the kitchen.

Situated in a small cottage, Chesney based his business model on one person handling the orders and the money. The first months at the initial Rockybilt at 906 East Colfax Avenue compelled Chesney to rethink that model: "After the first six months with the one on East Colfax Avenue I had made $90 profit." The ledger indicated that Chesney's salary of fifty dollars per month meant that these Rockys were soon to crumble if something drastic didn't happen.

"I knew I had to expand or quit," Chesney recalled, "so I borrowed money and opened one [restaurant] at W. 38th Avenue and Federal Boulevard and followed it with one on Santa Fe Drive."[84] Armed with his uncle's financial backing, the small cottages with the big name had grown to three locations by the end of the 1930s and had doubled again by the time America entered the Second World War in December 1941. Maybe not as catchy as "Have It Your Way" or "Where's the Beef?" the Rockybilts marketing come-on was, "Rockybilt builds HAMBURGERS—TAK-HOMA-SAK."[85]

The marketing strategy may have been a little suspect, but Chesney's food philosophy was to "buy the best": "If you won't eat it, or you won't serve it to a friend—don't serve it." During the war years, Rockybilts' most influential customer was Colorado governor Ralph Carr. Best known for his opposition to the vilification and the relocation of Japanese Americans to internment camps, Carr had a Rockybilt habit. Often, he and his driver went into the original counter on East Colfax and ordered bags of burgers.

Many Denverites hoped that the city would return to its provincial, prewar character. However, as the rest of the nation discovered the city, its isolation faded.

In 1951, Chesney celebrated the fifteenth anniversary of his brainchild at the twelve different Rockybilts. Claiming that he was too busy for the chain's tenth anniversary in 1946, Chesney promoted a fifteenth birthday bash that got more than its share of press. Opening at 10:00 a.m. on a hot July 16 and surrounded by a block-long crowd, the original Rockybilts store offered 1936 prices on the following specials: five-cent hamburgers, ten-cent cheeseburgers, nickel pies, and ten-cent pies *à la mode*. A breakfast of ham, two eggs, and toast went for twenty cents; bacon and eggs for fifteen cents; and steak sandwiches for ten cents.

The day started with four thousand buns, four hundred pounds of hamburgers, sixty-nine pies, and "great stacks of other food on hand," according to a day-after report in the *Denver Post*. The anniversary was special for Chesney. "It cost plenty but it was worth it. We lost a little on everything we sold and we sold plenty."[86]

Rockybilts had other famous fans. Rob Mohr and his family have been in Denver's restaurant supply business for nearly sixty years. He recalled enjoying a few Rockybilt hamburgers at a stand near the Auditorium Arena in downtown Denver in the late 1960s. Mid-bite, Mohr recalled his surprise at the arrival of professional wrestler "Haystacks" Calhoun. At six feet, four

Too busy to celebrate its tenth anniversary, the Rockybilt lowered prices on its birthday five years later in 1951. *From authors' collection.*

inches tall and 640 pounds, announcers introduced Calhoun as he entered the ring each weekend on television's *All-Star Wrestling* as "big enough to go bear hunting with a switch." Haystacks needed two stools to sit on before enjoying a pre-match snack. More relentless in a restaurant than he was in the ring, Calhoun quickly devoured more than his fair share of hamburgers.

On the day the first Rockybilt closed, Roy Chesney left the scene with a prophetic remark: "Today with so many places opened everywhere people aren't as conscious of Rockybilt as they once were. Truthfully, for a lot of years Denverites were very aware of Rockybilt."[87]

Mid-century Denver was a big enough hamburger town for the Rockybilts and other up-and-comers. Hi's Hamburgs had its moment on a bun from the late 1930s to the mid-1970s. Hiram (or Hyman) V. Plummer opened his first stand at 1731–33 Welton in 1939. By the mid-1950s, Plummer had locations at 617 16th Street and 2336 East 46th Avenue, an eastern outpost at 1247 East Colfax, and another at 1301 Broadway. Hi's covered the twenty-four-hour-a-day ground round trade. Denver resident Karen Zoltenko recalled that her favorite item was a fried egg and bacon sandwich topped with pickles on a hamburg(er) bun. One of the last locations, on the ground floor of the Howard Hotel at

Hello Hi's, it's almost time to say goodbye. The downtown Hi's Hamburgs awaits the wrecking ball at the Howard Hotel at 13ᵗʰ and Broadway in 1976. *From Tom Noel Photo Collection, Auraria Library, AUR-256.*

1301 South Broadway, measured twenty-eight by fifty feet. Hi's quietly said goodbye as Plummer's last stand fell to the wrecking ball in 1976. There is scant information on the Rockybilt's only rival for the city's hamburger crown.[88]

One surviving Rockybilt stands at 3275 South Broadway, sharing a parking lot with one of the city's oldest theaters, the Gothic. For longevity, the China Palace remained at this address longer than the original tenant did. A March 31, 1978 *Westword* review captured the atmosphere and the difference of ownership at this old Rockybilt: "Six seats overlook the three large woks where the food is cooked. You can eat in, and you will likely be sharing that space with a half dozen children belonging to the owners, who occasionally dash out to save their parking lot from cheap movie goers." Today, the last of the Rockybilts is a cluttered office associated with a barbecue chain a few feet to the south.[89]

Rockybilts Redux

By the mid-1980s, the red-and-white, six-seats-around-a-grill Rockybilt restaurants were gone. Still, the Rockybilt sandwich appeared in the most unusual places. A 1987 *Rocky Mountain News* article celebrating the fifty-second anniversary of the Humpty Dumpty and Denver's contribution to the myth of the cheeseburger contained a reference that neatly separated the old veterans from the newcomers when it came to Denver dining. As the grills smoked and the burgers sizzled, the reporter made mention of *Denver Post* columnist Dick Kreck putting some "lumpy pinkish goo that looked suspiciously like bottled Thousand Island dressing" on his burger.[90] The Rockybilt secret sauce still lived despite the observations of feckless journeymen reporters. In fact, the Rockybilts were enjoying a renaissance just a few blocks to the south of the cheeseburger's anniversary carnival.

The last Rockybilt, at Federal and Speer, closed in 1980. Just as the Rockybilt appeared to be lost to time, it reappeared at Micky Manor, a dive bar on Federal Boulevard. City councilman Dominic Coloroso established and operated Micky Manor in the 1940s, and its best-known visitor for a drink and some political chitchat was Vice President Hubert Humphrey.

The 1970s were not kind to Micky Manor or the surrounding neighborhood of Jefferson Park. Enter the next apostle of the Rockybilt sandwich faith: Ronnie Bay. Bay was a North High graduate, a Korean War veteran, and a friend of the Coloroso family. As family members began to pass away, the Colorosos turned to Bay to run the bar. At first Bay refused, but a visit to the Manor had him thinking in a few different directions. "I hadn't been there in years," Bay told the *Rocky Mountain News* in 1992, "and I couldn't believe it. It was frightening, like walking into this smoky den…a treacherous, threatening place. I went back to the Colorosos and said, 'I'm not tough enough to run that place.'"[91]

Bay eventually changed his mind and took over management of the place, but he also became the new sheriff of the Manor. For the first job on the list, Bay established a "no cussing" policy and fined customers when they let loose with a bad word. Like an episode of *Gunsmoke*, Bay realized that his strict but fair rule was going to work when he stopped a reprobate who started beating a woman. Every man in the bar came to Bay's defense and to help "eighty-six" the thug.

The nights spent wondering what would come next helped Bay make up his mind to buy Micky Manor in 1988. When Jerri and Richard Sanchez bought the place from Bay in 1996, Ronnie Bay retained rights to the "secret" Rockybilt sauce and sold it for fifty-one dollars per gallon to the Sanchezes.

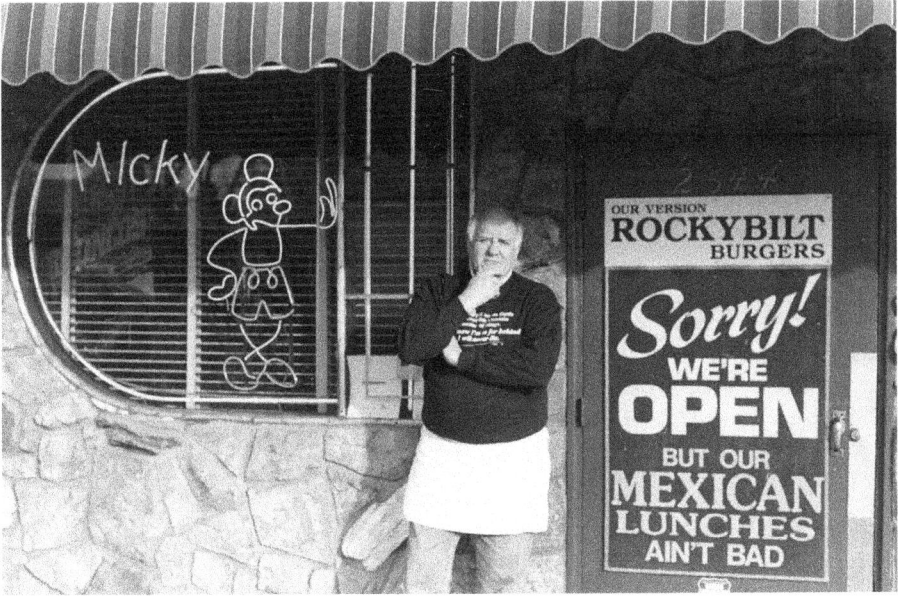

Owner Ronnie Bay holds down the fort at one of the last bastions of the Rockybilts, Micky Manor. *From Tom Noel Photo Collection, Auraria Library, AUR-394.*

More than three decades after the last scraping of grease from a Rockybilt grill, *Westword* writer Bill Gallo painted the following picture in late 2000: "The Rockybilt hamburger, a humble object of desire that sent three generations of Denverites into swoons of praise, has long gone the way of cocktails at the Shirley-Savoy, the Broncos' vertically striped socks, and convenient Stapleton Airport." Gallo concluded that Micky Manor remained "a classic, a cherished relic of Denver—whether or not Rockybilt nostalgia stirs your tastebuds and moves your soul."[92]

Bay died in June 2012. His obituary referred to this Marine Corps veteran and keeper of a house where ladies were welcomed and no bad language was tolerated as the "Friendly Giant of North Denver."[93]

AMERICAN GRAFFITI ON FEDERAL

As outlying bucolic farming communities evolved into metropolitan Denver, the bond between the automobile and hamburger also coalesced. In 1952, the onetime apple orchards and pasturelands of Arvada and Wheat Ridge counted three "Ins" (or "Inns"), Allen's, Hillcrest, and the Tip Top. Not to be outdone, the south end of town had the Hamburger Hut at 4605 South Santa Fe, and Lakewood's West Colfax Avenue featured Sellens Drive In at 9400 West Colfax and Fehr's at 6900 West Colfax. To the south, Littleton maintained the Thoroughbred theme established by Centennial Racetrack with the Horseshoe Drive Inn and the Paddock Drive Inn, both on South Santa Fe Drive.[94]

All evocative of the 1950s, none of these establishments made it to the twenty-first century. Over the next half century, food became faster and cars became dining rooms. On the roll call of Denver's lost drive-ins, one stands out in the memory for how it captured a generation of teenagers and sold their "who cares?" attitude right back at them.

In the basement of his home in suburban Denver, Carl Cerveny looked back almost forty years and realized that he was "fortunate" to run a drive-in during the era of kids and cruising. The kilt lifts on the Scotchman's story in 1949. Cerveny's uncle, Herman Christopher, opened the Frosted Scotchman between 48th and 49th and Federal, serving "San-a-Serv" ice cream. "He was of Germany ancestry," Cerveny recalled "but, he had red hair and everyone called him 'Chris.'" The plaid connection was born and took full flight as a jolly neon snowman in a kilt greeting customers along Federal Boulevard.[95]

At 4960 Federal Boulevard, the Scotchman Motor Restaurant (known by one and all as "the Scotchman") was the soundstage for Denver's version of *American Graffiti* from 1949 until 1977. Success came with the addition of hamburgers to the menu. A bent sense of humor also helped: "We used negative advertising—let's poke fun at the food...It was a farce," according to Cerveny. Lounging in your hot rod, a review of the Scotchman's menu included "Horribleburgers," "Choking Cokes," "Yur-pet Hot Dogs," and "Sloppy Malts." Signs at the restaurant jested, "Our food is horrible, so is the service," while the menu joked, "Our food is not touched by human hands. Our chef is a monkey." It wasn't above referring to another Denver institution by announcing that the Scotchman was "the Final Resting Place for Centennial Racehorses." No, *Mad Magazine*'s Alfred E. Neuman wasn't in the back cooking.[96]

The Hibernian snowman gave way to a neon lass in plaid above the declaration, "Open from 10 a.m. until exhausted." Uncle Chris passed away in 1953, leaving the Scotchman to Cerveny's mother and to Carl. The death of the founder didn't slow down the hijinks. For a number of years, the drive-in featured a wire cage with a sign that read, "old shoes for Horribleburger meat supply." Customers dropped off their used shoes and received a free

Oh, to be a kid again and cruise Federal. This decal showed the world that you had been to the Scotchman. *Courtesy of Carl Cerveny.*

ice cream cone. The shoes never made it to the meat grinder, but they did eventually find their way to a Native American reservation in Arizona.[97]

Flavored cokes were the rage during the golden era of the drive-in, but the Hot Kookie was one of a kind. The following is a recipe for a "Hot Kookie" (a 1950s nickname for a "hot chick," according to Mr. Cerveny). To try this at home, pour a cold "real thing" into a glass tumbler and ignore the bits about the ice and cola syrup.

Hot Kookie or Choking Coke (Courtesy of Carl Cerveny)

ice
go a little heavy with the Cola Syrup
a couple of drops of oil of Cassia delivered from an eyedropper
a couple of drops of red food coloring

Here is the flourish, what Mr. Cerveny calls "the sizzle on the steak." Insert a sipping straw into the concoction but don't stir, as it will mess up the look. As the Scotchman used to advise, "Sip it, don't straw it." If stirred, the oil of Cassia continues to increase the concoction's fiery flavor.[98]

Sloppy Malts and Hot Kookies. If only these old Scotchman cups could talk. *Courtesy of Carl Cerveny.*

Kids cruising downtown and back out to Federal Boulevard put the Scotchman on the map. "People would drive all night," said former carhop Linda Conner. "They'd go down 16th Street and then come up to the Scotchman. Then they'd go back down 16th Street and come back up to the Scotchman. When they found a parking spot, they'd have a Coke and maybe a burger and then go right back down 16th Street." Their orbit might also take them out to Colfax or South Broadway, but the Scotchman drew them back. Traffic lined up for blocks vying for one of the twenty-eight parking slots. "The prime spot was number 28, because if you parked facing south, you could see all the cars coming through," recalled Conner.

By the early 1970s, Cerveny had spotted a troubling change. His profit margin, which had always averaged about four cents on the dollar, began to shrink even though weekend nights were as busy as ever. Kids were still guzzling Coke, but they were buying fewer burgers. For decades, Americans enjoyed cheap gas to drive their big cars. By the early '70s, the price of gas had started climbing and sometimes was in short supply. The cost of filling up skyrocketed with the 1973 Arab oil embargo, leaving cruisers with less money for food. Compounding things, McDonald's, Burger King, and neighborhood residents aggravated by the cruising were also squeezing the fun out of running the Scotchman. With rising costs and dwindling nightly takes, Cerveny saw what was coming.

"The best thing in life is to know when you should stop," he said. Loyal customers were stunned when the drive-in announced that it was going to close. Cerveny described the evening of October 11, 1977, also Cerveny's birthday: "Everybody was waiting to see the Scotchman close. It was kind of like a wake. That lot was jam-packed. Across the street was a car wash, and there was a Der Weinerschintzel and a service station whose lots were also full. When we finally turned off the lights, everybody blew their horns."[99]

The Scotchman made a reappearance at Bandimere Speedway near Golden in 2006. Cerveny was on hand as middle-aged men in their chopped, cherry rides waited two hours for a Horribleburger and for a chance to go back to briefly revisit their youth. Looking back on that particular day, Cerveny reflected, "You don't remember what you were doing at thirty-five. You remember your first car, going to the prom, your first girlfriend. Being a teenager is a time of life everybody can relate to."[100]

As the Rockybilt chain and the Scotchman reached their respective ends, the '70s saw a larger trend that changed how the nation tasted its hamburgers. Marketing became just as important as asking if you wanted fries with that shake.

DIAL-A-BURGER

Round the Corner allowed diners to reach out and touch their hamburgers through the miracle of a short phone call. Reflecting how most Denverites—like their fellow citizens across the land—lived during the 1970s and 1980s, the majority of the fourteen or so Round the Corners were all in proximity to the metro area's shopping centers. Thirty years on, the following list reads like a memorial. Killed: Westminster, Cinderella City, and Aurora Mall. Wounded (or altered): Westland, Boulder's Crossroads Mall, Southwest Plaza, Southglenn, and Buckingham Square.

Perhaps an uncle of fast-casual restaurant marketing, Round the Corner was memorable for the toppings that a customer could add to his or her burger. Mustard, catsup and mayo were at the ready, but the slightly more adventurous suburbanite could order other combinations. The Pizza Burger was "a leaning tower of pizza cheese, secret sauce and lean charbroiled beef." The Burger Stroganoff, with mushrooms and a dollop of sour cream, really dressed up the humble patty. The Burger Especial came with guacamole, lettuce, grated cheese, "zesty pork green chili," and, yes, sour cream. Not everybody was sold. The May 19, 1972 *Rocky Mountain News* judged Round

Your hamburger is only one phone call away. Round the Corner was located near every Front Range mall during the 1970s and 1980s. *From Menu Collection, WH1509, Western History Collection, Denver Public Library.*

the Corners as "glorified hamburger establishments where some way out ideas have become standard fare."[101]

In 1992, Round the Corner downsized into today's Good Times. It became a drive-thru hamburger chain where phones were out and speaking to the box was in. The reasoning behind the change was simple, according to then executive vice-president of finance Boyd Hoback: "McDonald's and other chains say that 60 percent to 70 percent of their business is take-out, so there's a huge market out there. [Good Times] is really getting back to the basics of the hamburger business."[102]

Good Times directs about forty franchisees in Denver and Wyoming. On its menu is the Bambino, a slightly smaller single patty topped with what tastes quite a bit like Thousand Island dressing. The Bambino resembles Denver's most beloved hamburger, the Rockybilt. Therefore, what was a city's favorite hamburger many years ago lives again through the memories, and marketing, of the latest local hamburger chain. Good Times is not the only current Denver-based restaurant to celebrate the little square burgers. In the cozy confines of Nick's Café in Golden, a patty triple the size of the original Rockybilt goes by the name of the Rocky Burger.

Another stray sizzle from Denver's hamburger heritage is the short-lived and seldom remembered Sliders and Nails. Sliders (hamburgers) and Nails (French fries) attempted to re-create the madness of White Castle hamburgers. Ownership had two locations (2701 West Alameda Avenue in Lakewood and 2680 East Colfax Avenue in Aurora), as well as a thirty-one-cent hamburger and a 1975 Rolls-Royce Silver Shadow to make bulk deliveries. What Sliders and Nails did not have was capital, and it was out of business by September 1983—a year and a half after opening.[103]

The hamburger has undergone an interesting dietary and promotional renaissance since the 1990s. The beef industry spent part of the mid-twentieth century breeding cattle that looked (and were) leaner to compete with the purported health advantages of chicken and the "other white meat." Two decades ago, the horror stories surrounding *E. coli* bacteria and, subsequently, mad cow disease only pushed the marketing masterminds to re-create hamburgers as gourmet treats—at prices higher than those available from the prevalent national chains. Denver's SmashBurger; Washington, D.C.'s Five Guys; and, to a lesser degree, Southern California's In-N-Out Burgers display a variety of toppings and describe feeding regiments of contented cows unaware of their fates. These newer chains have more of a restaurant feel and, in the process, created a slightly slower version of fast food.

BACK TO THE NEIGHBORHOOD

"Sure I got a recipe. But I don't give my recipe to nobody." So spoke Dominic Carbone from Carbone's Italian Sausage House at 1221 West 38th Avenue in March 1975. In the mid-1970s, Dominic had been in the sausage business for sixteen years and kept his grandfather's "formula" in a safety deposit box.[104] It's a north Denver thing. You wouldn't understand.

Language is a funny thing. Most of the world familiar with Italian cooking knows that a cannoli is a fried pastry crust resembling a pipe, with a sweet mascarpone filling. Mixed inside the filling are chocolate chips, candied fruit, pistachios, or some other sweet treat. Since the mid-twentieth century, and among a handful of restaurants in a limited number of blocks of north Denver, a canoli has meant something more substantial.

Associated with many Italian American restaurants in north Denver, Lechuga's still features the snack known by many names—the canoli. *Photo by Robert Autobee.*

At the start of this examination, we looked at the unchanging nature of north Denver's family-owned restaurants. As the second decade of the twenty-first century got underway, the Italian community in north Denver, and the rest of the city, lost one of its long-established and well-loved institutions: Carbone's Italian Sausage House. The Carbone family was behind one of the great menu mysteries in the city's dining history: why did they call a chunk of Italian sausage wrapped with a chile pepper and a strip of cheese encased in bread dough a canoli? The canoli is called a "Tutty Toots" at Lechuga's (the successor to Carbone's on Tejon Street) or, with an extra jalapeño, a Lil' Bambino, or even a Sassy Patsy's at Patsy's Inn on Navajo Street.

Patsy's Inn owner, Ron Cito, remembered back more than sixty years ago, when his mother baked bread in a hearth in their backyard. "She would trade bread for other food," Cito recalled. The big Friday treat for good Catholic Italian families was a thick, chewy bread dough smothered with sauce and cheese and maybe duck, quail, or chicken—but no beef. Cito believes that the canoli is related to the traditional Italian holiday dish Pizza Rustica, or Easter Pie.[105]

The son of a Denver police officer, Nick Andurlakis grew up in north Denver and knew all the neighborhood characters. As a precocious teenager, he heard the story of the likely birth of the canoli from its most likely father, Richard Carbone. Andurlakis recalled the conversation he had decades

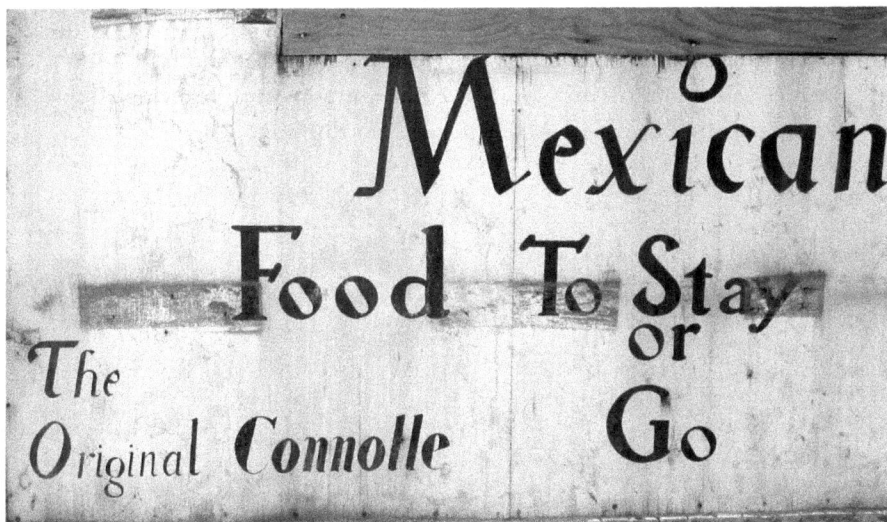

Longo's Subway also featured canolis. Same treat, different spelling. *Photo by Robert Autobee.*

earlier that when Carbone made square pizzas, he trimmed the edges of the dough to the size of the pan. Not one to waste anything, Carbone wrapped the extra dough around pieces of his famous sausage. So perhaps this north Denver treat also got its name from its resemblance to a pipe.[106]

Upon closing Longo's Subway Tavern in the late summer of 2012, owner Barb Longo told *Westword* that her father-in-law, Ray, "designed the calzone, but we call it a canoli." The nomenclature for this humble treat at Longo's covered all the various spellings—cannoli, canoli, and connolle. Whatever you want to call it, here is one quick version of this simple delicacy.

North Denver Canoli

pizza dough or frozen bread dough
Italian mild, sweet, or hot sausage (depending on your mood), cut in lengths about 2
*   inches long*
jalapeño strips or green pepper (depending on your mood)
small ½-inch slices of mozzarella or provolone cheese
your favorite Mariana sauce

Boil Italian sausage in hot water. Remove sausage when the water reaches a rolling boil. Remove the sausage casing. Spread flat enough dough to surround the sausage. Arrange a pepper strip, a slice of cheese, and a piece of sausage on the dough; roll; and then seal the dough on the long edge, just covering the ends. Arrange canoli on a sheet and bake at 425 degrees Fahrenheit in an oven for 20 minutes or until brown on top. Serve hot out of oven with Mariana sauce for dipping.

CHAPTER 4

Migrating Tastes

DENVER GOES METROPOLITAN

A city with returning servicemen housed in chicken coops. A flood of new families unable to find places to live. Rationing of essentials such as beef, sugar, and butter. Only a few restaurants not serving uninspired cuisine. If that wasn't bad enough, only 30 percent of the city's restaurants were fit to eat in. No, it wasn't one of the great capitals of postwar Europe. It was Denver in the months following VJ Day. However, the city had enough promise and potential for those stationed at Fitzsimmons and Lowry, as well as those war workers cranking out shells at Remington Arms Plant in Lakewood. Peacetime prosperity ushered in seemingly unending migration to the Mile High City that continues to this day.

In those first months of peace, the city's diners could trust old standbys like Joe "Awful" Coffee's Ringside Lounge and Eddie Bohn's Pig 'n' Whistle for steak, spaghetti, or fried shrimp. As more people visited the Rockies or made homes in Denver, a more refined approach to dining followed. Restaurants like Pierre Wolfe's Quorum and Le Profile continued formal dining as Americans became more casual in their public dress—a suit and tie for the gentlemen and hats, heels, and gloves for the ladies. This would eventually change as the restaurant industry embraced trends emphasizing showmanship over satisfaction.

Pawnshops, shot-and-beer places, and lost souls now populated Denver's original restaurant district between Larimer and Lawrence and 19th and 20th Streets. The heart of Old Denver was undergoing a transition. It was the scene for an unusual postwar migration for Japanese Americans held

A girl with a camera was a fixture of many American restaurants during the mid-twentieth century. This souvenir photo folder comes from a night out at Boggio's. *Accession #2009.76.2, History Colorado, Denver, Colorado.*

A souvenir photo from Boggio's, signed by the men in the photo, with the note, "E.J. Chas. Hicks the Best Waiter in Denver." *Accession #2009.76.2, History Colorado, Denver, Colorado.*

Boggio's Parisienne Rotisserie - Tremont at Broadway - Denver, Colorado

"Recommended by Leading Stage, Screen and Radio Celebrities"

Owner Nate Boggio rode to Cheyenne Frontier Days with Bob Hope once. Maybe that's where the recommendation on the postcard came from. *From authors' collection.*

in internment camps. From 1945 to 1947, internees made their way to Denver from the intermountain west camps. Japanese were not allowed to return to the West Coast immediately after the camps closed. Denver was behind only Chicago in the number of Japanese Americans waiting to return to the Pacific Coast. While waiting in Denver, several ex-internees briefly ran restaurants in the area later known as Sakura Square. They joined well-established Japanese restaurants like Fred's Meshi-Ya (owned by Fred Aoki) at 1953 Larimer and the Chop Suey Tea Room at 1223 20th Street. Others, like Mansei-An (which advertised that it was from Los Angeles in Denver's Japanese newspaper, *Rocky Shimpo*), at 2104 Larimer Street; the Nikkow Low at 2038 Larimer; and the Quick Lunch owned by Isami Yoshikawa made a quick entrance before going out of business or leaving to go home to the West Coast to rebuild their prewar lives.[107]

The years between 1945 and 1965 brought as much change to Denver as any two-decade span since the 1859 gold rush. First, the city doubled in population from approximately 300,000 in 1930 to nearly 600,000 in 1960. This period of suburbs, shopping centers, and big cars also represents a transitional moment in how Denverites—and all Americans—ate.

CLEAN UP YOUR ACT

By the late 1940s, conditions hadn't improved much from four decades earlier, when the flies outnumbered customers in some Denver restaurants. Around Thanksgiving 1947, the United States Public Health Service findings filled Denver's newspapers, noting that unacceptable sanitation existed in nearly 70 percent of the city's restaurants and cafés. On a scale of 100, no Denver restaurant ranked above 77 percent. The lowest came in at 13 percent; 98 percent of Denver's restaurants failed to meet the basic disease control requirement to place a sign in the toilets notifying employees that no person with a communicable disease should work in any restaurant. The survey determined that the cleaning and storage of utensils did not meet an expected standard of cleanliness.

Over the next few years, fines and negative attention convinced local restaurateurs to spend an estimated $2 million for improving and modernizing facilities and equipment. Ruth Bennett's eponymous café north of downtown served mechanics, cops, and neighbors hamburgers, oxtail soup, and malts. Bennett's daughter, Ruth Bradford, turned 102 in the summer of 2014. She recalled, "We always passed inspection—Thank God." Bennett's granddaughter, Rose Ann Taht, did not recall a dishwasher in the kitchen, but there were three sinks—washing, rinsing, and the final rinse. Both ladies mused that if the city's health inspectors had their closed their café, both they and their neighbors would have had to find a new lunch spot. By 1955, the city's restaurants had regained some dignity, and diners gained some peace of mind as city health officials recorded that 79 percent of the Denver's restaurants were clean enough to eat in.[108]

THE BOXER AND THE ARCHITECTS

Joe "Awful" Coffee was a Colorado state boxing champion in the bantam and featherweight categories after the First World War. "Awful" was a reference to how his punches felt for his opponents. Coffee left the ring to start his Ringside Lounge at 1120 17th Street in 1943. For the next twenty-three years, the Ringside's atmosphere and menu was much like the city itself after the war: basic, with items like spaghetti with chicken ravioli for $0.90 and grilled Virginia ham steak with pineapple rings for $1.50.

Joe Coffee's Ringside Lounge was B. Kent Lloyd's meal before his pre-induction physical during World War II. It's noted in his souvenir menu. *From Menu Collection, WH1509, Western History Collection, Denver Public Library.*

Joe "Awful" Coffee could throw a mean uppercut, and his bartender could mix a cocktail with a punch. *From Menu Collection, WH1509, Western History Collection, Denver Public Library.*

The owners of the Tiffin Inn in Capitol Hill were the "Architects of Appetites" and the poobahs of promotion. *From authors' collection.*

One of the first postwar Denver restaurants that sought to re-create a continental menu and atmosphere was the Tiffin Inn. Jean and Paul Shank, the self-proclaimed "Architects of Appetites," renovated a Capitol Hill mansion at 1600 Odgen Street. Their 1940s menus featured entrées like casserole of braised tenderloin tips with mushrooms and breast of Dakota ring neck pheasant under glass.

Soon the Shanks gained a national reputation through a review by nationally known *boulevardier* Lucius Beebe. In the October 1948 *Gourmet* magazine, Beebe patted Denver on its head as "a town of many excellences but one never notable as a shrine of gastronomy." Regardless, he praised the Tiffin: "The Tiffin Inn is a symposium of beefy wonderments, juicy, thick beef tenderloins, boneless New York–cut sirloins, choice boneless club steaks, double-cut prime sirloins, and the house specialty, the Tiffin famous double filet, served for one with French-fried onion rings, $3.50."

Beebe had one gripe as he waited for the Burlington Zephyr to take him back to Manhattan: "This department personally could do without the liking of the management in its fonder moments to think of itself as 'architects of appetite,' but this is inconsequential, and our empathic cup of tea, to scramble a phrase, is the Tiffin's double filet with French-fried onions. Boy! It is something!"[109]

Home Is Everything

Beebe never made it to the Auraria neighborhood during his 1948 visit. He would have found the recently opened restaurant, Casa Mayan, more intriguing than the Tiffin. The Casa Mayan story began in El Paso, Texas, with the birth in 1894 of Carolina Acuña Diaz, who married Ramon Gonzàlez seventeen years later. Like other Anglo- or Mexican Americans, the proximity of the Mexican Revolution drove the Gonzàlez family north, finally arriving in Denver in 1919. Early twentieth-century Denver was not the Jim Crow South, but Marta Gonzàlez, Ramon and Carolina's daughter, recalled that those with brown skin were not always made to feel welcome. "I remember her saying that she and my father were going 'across the creek' into [downtown] Denver. They went to a restaurant where somebody said that my father looked white, but my mom looked too Mexican. They didn't go in."[110]

Making their way the best they could in a city where some restaurants posted "No Mexicans or Dogs" signs, the Gonzàlezes eventually settled in the west side neighborhood of Auraria. The Gonzàlez house at 1020 9th Street soon became a beacon to lost souls suffering from the Depression of the 1930s. The rail yard was near their house, and word got around that anybody "living rough" could receive a meal by knocking on their door. "We never turned anyone down," Gonzàlez recalled.

The 1930s Auraria neighborhood was a mingling and melting pot of cultures. The family's generous and helpful nature earned Ramon the nickname "Gonzàlesteen" from their Jewish neighbors. In 1946, they decided to open a restaurant, Casa Mayan, in their home. Suspicions rooted in ethnic stereotypes contributed to a rough start. Marta Gonzàlez recalled that the City and County of Denver ordered a command performance in their kitchen to ensure "sanitary" conditions. They need not have worried, as Carolina Gonzàlez was a nurse, and those who worked in the kitchen "scrubbed their hands. She was very fussy." That did not stop officials from ruling from their prejudices. "The city's health officers had a hard time with our tamales. Traditionally, we would spread the *masa*, the corn meal surrounding the meat of the tamale, on cornhusks. They wanted us to use paper instead. We had a big battle over that."[111]

Casa Mayan's innovations quickly captured the attention of the adventurous. Preparation was labor intensive, and dishes like Denver's

Carolina and Ramon Gonzàlez get ready to serve up another chile relleno plate. Casa Mayan popularized chile rellenos and guacamole tostadas. *Courtesy of Gregorio Alcaro.*

first chile rellenos and guacamole tostadas were made from scratch. Arnie Gonzàlez visited a Mexican village where the locals ate "something that looked like pizza"—hence the tostada. Open from 5:00 p.m. to 10:00 p.m., Ramon marked the day's bill of fare on a chalkboard. So that the customers could taste a little of everything, the Gonzàlezes offered small portions of several dishes on a plate: enchiladas, tacos, tamales, and rice and beans—what today we would call a combination plate. The family's chile relleno recipe is from the *Denver Post's Empire Magazine* in 1957. Nearly sixty years later, Carolina's grandson Gregorio Alcaro admitted that his family softened the "exotic" nature of this recipe so it would reach a wider audience in the *Post*'s Sunday magazine section.

Chile Rellenos

½ medium-sized onion, finely chopped	1 tablespoon shortening
½ cup water	2 cups tomato sauce
½ teaspoon salt	4 large eggs, separated
½ cup lard	4 California peeled green chiles (medium hot)
¼ pound American cheese	2 tablespoons flour

Brown onion in shortening. Add water and tomato sauce. Bring to boil. Reduce heat and simmer gently while preparing chiles. Add salt to egg whites and beat until stiff. Beat egg yolks slightly and gently fold in egg whites. Blend thoroughly.

Heat skillet on low to medium heat; add lard. Remove seeds from chiles, being careful not split the pepper. Canned chiles, incidentally, are the easiest to use. If fresh chiles are used, they must first be roasted, and the skin must be removed. Cut cheese into slices a quarter-inch thick and two inches long. Stuff chiles with cheese. Sprinkle chiles with flour. Increase skillet heat until lard is hot. Dip chiles in egg batter and then place in skillet. Cover entire chile with batter and put immediately into the hot lard. Cook until browned on both sides. Serve each covered with hot tomato sauce. Makes 4.[112]

Big local names and international figures found their way to the Gonzàlez *casa*. Judy Collins, Helen Bonfils, and Mary Chase (author of *Harvey*) all sampled the Casa Mayan's tamales and *arroz y frijoles* (rice and beans). Students, artists, and dancers also made Casa Mayan their home. Sometimes a nightly parade of food and frivolity caused Marta Gonzàlez to wonder, "I had some doubts if it was my house." During the 1948 presidential campaign, Harry Truman stopped by. As a young man, Sam Arnold, future restaurant impresario and creator of The Fort Restaurant, begged the family to let him wash dishes so he could observe the preparation of the delicacies from behind a cloud of soapsuds. Marta Gonzàlez fondly remembers flamenco guitarist Carlos Montoya coming for a meal in the late 1940s.[113]

Cooking brought together what would seem like wildly different cultures. The Gonzàlez family worked with local Japanese farmers to plant traditional varieties of chiles, beans, and corn that were the essence of Casa Mayan's burritos and enchiladas. This tasty exchange went both ways. Restaurateur Leo Goto recounted that as a kid growing up in Denver he traded "rice balls and pickled fish for burritos" with the Mexican kids he knew.[114]

Good food and good times troubled those in power with hateful attitudes and unadventurous palates. Gonzàlez and her son, Gregorio Alcaro, recalled

It's 9:40 p.m. on some half-remembered night in the early '60s. The party was often going at Casa Mayan many evenings over three decades. *Courtesy of Gregorio Alcaro.*

that there were those with unpopular political opinions and members of social action groups, like the League of United Latin American Citizens (LULAC), who ate at Casa Mayan. They played chess with Ramon, danced, listened to music, and discussed how to improve the lives of Denver's Mexican and Mexican American population. Alcaro compared the atmosphere at Casa Mayan to Denver's modern outpost of free thinking, the Mercury Café. For these suspicious activities, the Federal Bureau of Investigation (FBI) watched Casa Mayan for a time, but there is no record if it ever ordered anything to go. As a testimony that good food can bridge differences, Casa Mayan grew to feed an overwhelming number of Anglos seduced by the spell cast by rice and beans, chorizo, and chile rellenos. However, this act of gastronomic goodwill had some in the Mexican American community wondering if the Gonzàlez family had sold out.

Progress has no taste or feeling. Such was the case when Casa Mayan closed to accommodate the expansion of the Auraria Higher Education Center. As a youngster, Gregorio Alcaro helped prepare for the restaurant's "Last Supper" on Halloween Night 1973. "The place was just packed," he stated some forty years later. "We finally closed on November 1, which is the Day of the Dead, an important spiritual day for most Mexicans. It wasn't planned; it just happened that way."[115] The family felt that Casa Mayan was too special to relocate. The current family matriarch, Marta Gonzàlez, who turned ninety shortly after her interview, advises that anybody in the restaurant business should consider and follow how her family ran—and lived—Casa Mayan. "If you don't have heart, you don't have good food."[116]

BREAKFAST FOR LUNCH...AND DINNER

From tortillas to pancakes, other Denver families were successful in cooking and serving the dishes of their respective cultures. Another longtime favorite of many Denverites—and one of our nation's presidents—was Lund's Swedish Pancake House at 1817 18th Street. Immigrating from Småland province in southern Sweden, John Lund Sr. opened a restaurant in Denver in 1911. Lund's brother, Gus, had arrived the year before and was working at the Lewis Hotel at 1835 Champa. John worked at a meatpacking plant for a year before he decided to open a restaurant featuring Lund's family recipe for pancakes. Lund's dream started in the 900 block of 14th Street before moving on to 1817 Champa in 1920. Dating to 1870, the building's back room stood on "charred timbers...and brick," and the restaurant seated sixty people.

Holly Arnold Kinney, owner of The Fort Restaurant, recalled how much she liked the pancakes and sausage. Other high-profile regulars included the judges from the nearby federal district court. On one occasion, a national conference of U.S. Circuit Courts of Appeals judges selected Lund's for a pancake luncheon. In 1957, Lund Sr. died, and the business transferred to his son, John Jr. In 1958, the family went national with their pancake mix. President Dwight D. Eisenhower used the mix on a summer visit to Fraser. Later, the chief executive wrote to John Lund Jr. describing his "fine success" with the pancakes.

Lund's changed as the 1960s came in, and the old building gave out. In 1961, Lund's moved next door to the corner of 18th and Champa. The family tried to duplicate their success in the suburbs. In 1967, a second store opened on West Colfax in Lakewood. The last day for Lund's downtown was a Saturday in late February 1970. The *Rocky Mountain News* recalled that "[o]ld customers missed the uneven floors, the old wooden booths, and the crowded quarters of the old place." For almost six decades, fans have found Lund's Swedish Pancake Mix in supermarkets across the country.[117]

BLARNEY'S PARADOX

A teetotaling Irishman bought whiskey in hundred-bottle lots and introduced the city to "Irish coffee." Then he launched Denver's current St. Patrick's Day parade—on April 17, when the Lord Mayor of Dublin was visiting. Before corporate commercialization of Celtic culture, Bernard J. Duffy opened two Irish bar-restaurants: Duffy's Tavern on Champa in 1950 and, later in 1956, Duffy's Shamrock on 1635 Court Place, which became the best known. Junior newsroom staff from the *Rocky Mountain News* swear that Duffy's was the best place for a corned beef sandwich and potato salad when leaving the newspaper offices around midnight.

Duffy was in the hospitality business for more than two decades before he sold his Shamrock to Frank and Ken Lombardi in 1963. Experienced with pickled customers, Duffy went to work for a local mortuary only to open Duffy's Cherry Cricket in 1968. Frank and Ken Lombardi held on to the Shamrock for almost forty years despite the annual St. Patrick's Day madness. After patrons broke into the kitchen and started a pie fight and two naked customers danced down the seventy-foot-long bar, the Lombardis closed Duffy's on St. Patrick's Day from 1984 to 1992 and then closed for good in 2006. For better or worse, these things do not happen at Bennigan's every March 17.[118]

Highballs and Chow Mein

Next to a 1948 editorial about President Truman battling with Congress, *Rocky Mountain News* editor Jack Foster extolled the wonders of the recently opened Lotus Room. The Lotus Room was the city's shining palace of Americanized Cantonese Chinese food for forty years. Foster left the Lotus Room ebullient after his first visit: "You've never tasted anything like it. There's something about Chinese cooking that gives you a feeling of luxurious eating that you cannot get from any other kind of food." With so many options today, it is hard to imagine the "exoticness" of sweet and sour, and fried Chinese food. The 1954 menu's Mandarin family-style dinner for six people cost twelve dollars and offered a feast of "fried rice, egg foo young, pineapple sweet and sour boneless pork, Cantonese lobster or almond duck, fried won ton, subgum or chicken chowmein, lotus royal sundaes, and almond cookies." Of course, all dinners included egg rolls, fried prawns, tea, and soup. By 1978, the price of this dinner had doubled.[119]

The Fongs—first Esther and Frank and, later, son Bob—ran the Lotus Room. Memories of the Lotus Room are bathed in eerie neon reds and yellows from the adjoining Veterans of Foreign Wars (VFW) bar. Thousands of Denver families have happy recollections of the Lotus Room, but Jack Foster was clearly the restaurant's biggest fan. Future *Rocky Mountain News* editor Michael Balfe Howard was entirely complimentary in recalling a dinner at the Lotus Room after accepting a job as general assignment reporter at the *News* in the mid-1960s:

> *We cemented our deal for me to become a general assignment reporter in August 1965 by celebrating at the Lotus Room. Few today in Denver have ever heard of the Lotus Room, I imagine; if your taste runs in the direction of greasy mutton fat washed down by Sake-tinis (Sake and vodka) you were probably in the right place. Sharing space with the V.F.W. on Bannock Street and Speer Boulevard, the Lotus Room had it all, from gambling at Chinese New Year's with the mayor to the best egg roll in town. The price was right, too.*[120]

HOME OF
John S. Stewart
Post No. 1.
"Original Post of"
VETERANS OF FOREIGN WARS OF THE U. S.
Speer Blvd. and 9th Ave.
DENVER, COLORADO

THE LOTUS ROOM

ENTRANCE TO COCKTAIL LOUNGE

After the war, the Lotus Room in the VFW post at 9th and Bannock reintroduced Chinese food to Denver. *From authors' collection.*

The Lotus Room closed in the early 1990s. Through the mists of time, an ocean of vegetable oil, and Mr. Howard's recommendation comes the recipe for the Lotus Room egg roll.

Lotus Room Egg Rolls

3 eggs
1 teaspoon salt
½ pound beef or pork
2 teaspoons soy sauce
2 teaspoons dry sherry
½ teaspoon ground ginger
2 teaspoons cornstarch
3 tablespoons chopped onion
3 tablespoons flour
3 tablespoons water
vegetable oil for frying
6 egg pancakes or egg roll wrappers

Beat the eggs with ½ teaspoon salt. Pour about 2 tablespoons into a hot, greased 6-inch skillet, tilting the pan quickly. Fry until lightly browned and set. Repeat with remaining eggs. You should have six egg pancakes or sheets. Combine the ground meat, soy sauce, sherry, ginger, cornstarch, onion, and remaining salt and mix thoroughly. Divide meat mixture among the egg sheets. Turn opposite sides in and roll up. Seal edges with the flour mixed with the water. Heat the oil to 370 degrees Fahrenheit and fry the rolls until browned. Drain the rolls and cut crosswise on the bias into three pieces each. Serve hot, with mixed salt and pepper for dipping or with mustard. Serves 6.[121]

FUJI EN

SPECIALIZING in SUKIYAKI, TEMPURA

※一二〇名様まで
※パーテイ歓迎
ビール
日本酒
天ぷら
※すきやき
ご注文下さい
多少にかゝわらず
二弗五十仙より
付き・お一人様・
持ち帰り用風呂敷
※二重ね折詰料理

日本料理

お引受けます
いつでも
宴会パーテイ
より十時まで
日曜―午後四時
午前一時まで
月曜より土曜まで
午后四時より
休業なし

富士園

930 LINCOLN ST., DENVER, 266-2178

The Fuji En kept Japanese food on the radar for local diners in the days before sushi grew in popularity across Denver. *From* Rocky Mountain Jiho, *January 8, 1969.*

At the Fuji En, a bridge led to tables where you removed your shoes before reviewing a menu filled with teriyaki and tempura. *From authors' collection.*

Perhaps the best-remembered Japanese restaurant between 1946 and the 1980s was outside the city's traditional Japanese enclave between Lawrence and Larimer Streets. The Fuji En at 930 Lincoln was a miniature, idealized version of Japan. Established in 1959, it was Denver's only Japanese restaurant for most Denverites. A miniature wooden bridge led diners to the main dining room or to one of the "Zashiki Tea Rooms"—small areas along the dining room that were divided by sliding shoji doors and required removal of shoes before entering. The menu was not foreign by today's

吉田喜 ●豆腐卸し店 栄養と健康 湯どうふ 〒 TOFU CO. Phone 623-5031 2430 Larimer St., Denver デンバ豆腐店

Mandarin Cafe 日本料理 マンダリン ▲パーテイにもご利用下さい ※中華料理 鍋焼うどん すきやき 天ぷら ▲日本料理 自慢のてりやき ビール 1221 - 20TH ST., DENVER 244-9526

The Mandarin Café survived Larimer's postwar decline by serving some Japanese dishes and a lot of Chinese main courses. *From* Rocky Mountain Jiho, *January 8, 1969.*

standards—teriyaki, shrimp tempura, and sukiyaki—but a visit to the Fuji En was as Far East as Denver got during the 1960s and 1970s.[122]

Denver's Japanese neighborhood around 19th and Larimer remained the home of stalwarts like Fred's Place (later Akebono's) and the 20th Street Café. Fred and Chiyeko Aoki opened Fred's Place at 1953 Larimer in 1942. The couple changed the name to Akebono (Japanese for "dawn") in 1960. On the corner of 20th and Larimer, beneath a neon sign advertising "Chop Suey," the Tani family served Chinese (and, subsequently, Japanese) food at the Mandarin Café for many years.

Aurora's Apple Tree Shanty played up the ethnic angle—in this case, an idealized Netherlands—at 8710 East Colfax from 1949 to 1992. The Shanty cooked most of its entrées on an apple wood grill behind the main restaurant. Beef tenderloin tips seared in a cast aluminum apple mold with a removable lid were the Shanty's specialty. Once the wood fire reached four hundred degrees, the cook stuffed the tips into the mold and covered it with the lid. The entrée reached the diner medium rare and still in the mold. Beloved by Aurora and many out-of-state visitors heading east on U.S. Highway 40, not everybody was captivated. The critic for the *Rocky Mountain Business Journal* rained on the parade with comments of "cornball" surroundings, "well-drilled" waitresses who curtsied to the customer after the bill was settled, "nondescript" salads, and a crowd that "looked like it came from Furr's [Cafeteria]." Other than that, we can only suspect that the reviewer had a good time.[123]

ELSEWHERE ON EAST COLFAX

Unfortunately, Lucien Broch is a forgotten name in this town. From France, Broch family members were chefs going back to his grandfather. In 1952, Broch renovated an old bungalow at East Colfax and Eudora and called it the Normandy. Then he went back into the kitchen, put on his chef's toque, and prepared frog legs Provençal, chicken en cocotte grand-mère, or wiener schnitzel. Broch apologized beforehand for any delays in the meals. "I am just enough artist that I will not let food sit upon a steam table to be dished up as the customer desires. I will fix it fresh on order. If it takes a little time—well." His staff—Joseph from Paris and Jeanette from Marseille— probably wondered what they had gotten themselves into when they arrived in Denver to work in the restaurant.[124] It would take nearly another decade before Denver diners were again ready to leave steak for entrées with "à la" in their titles.

A BUCCANEER BATTLES ON LARIMER

A buccaneer is one who breaks the rules and plunders when necessary. The definition applies to Lafitte's. It opened on Larimer Street when it was still skid row and ten years away from the commercial renaissance brought by historic preservationist Dana Crawford. A handful of dark episodes led to the restaurant's demise some twenty years later. None involved an owner retiring or dying. It was racism, taxes, and perhaps a slight touch of arrogance.

In 1959, Joe Sperte and his son, Roger, offered their take on New Orleans–style cooking with an oyster bar and the downstairs décor reminiscent of

Denver, circa 1875. Because Larimer was still enduring its endless midnight of seediness, Laffite's may have been the first restaurant in Denver to offer valet parking.[125]

It took a few years, yet there he was—tiny in a one- by three-inch newspaper ad but big enough to boast—"The Man Who Brought Gourmet to Denver." His friend and competitor Pierre Wolfe described him as a "tough, cigar-smoking, hard-drinking restaurateur."[126] Joe Sperte began his restaurant management career at Green Gables Country Club. The family of Sperte's partner, Marvin Cook, owned the three-story structure previously used as a plumbing supply warehouse. Cook told the *Denver Post* in December 1960 that "we (he and Sperte) believe in the revitalization of Larimer St. and the entire lower downtown area."[127] Wolfe later concurred that Lafitte's was very much an outpost on skid row and that if "additional help was needed to scrub pots and pans or mop the kitchen floor during the busy evening, Roger [Sperte] simply walked out onto Larimer Street and offered a few hours of work to a yet-sober wanderer."[128]

Red-flocked wallpaper, red leather booths, and black-stained wood transformed the interior of the old building. A wide central stairway led to the oyster bar. The ladies' room featured golden swan faucets. The menu was also filled with promise—sixty different seafood dishes, with all creatures of the deep making their first and last journey to the Rockies via jet to Stapleton Airport. The menu revealed surprises like Monterey abalone steak sauté bercy and shad roe sautéed with bacon, herbs, and capers on toast points, or flounder with Chablis sauce and pompano en papillote. This second entrée was from Antoine's in New Orleans and combines pompano with shrimps, mushrooms, crabmeat, and scallops in a wine sauce. In a town satisfied with a good steak, Lafitte's arrived as a revelation.[129]

Good reviews and a happy clientele weren't enough. Changing times caught up with Lafitte's in 1965. On October 9, Roger Sperte refused to show George and Rose Mary Brown to a table even though the Browns held a reservation. The Browns waited in the restaurant's vestibule as several other patrons, some without reservations, were seated. George Brown was a state senator from Denver, and he and his wife were African American. The Browns took their complaint against Lafitte's to the Colorado Civil Rights Commission. The following July, in its first decision since its 1957 creation, the commission supported the Browns' charge and ordered Lafitte's management to make available "to all persons within the jurisdiction of the state of Colorado full and equal enjoyment."[130] Times indeed had changed. Richard Pinhorn's Manhattan decades earlier could and did advertise bigotry in the newspaper. Sixty years later, a court informed Laffite's to get with the times and serve everybody regardless of color.

By 1975, the buccaneer's sword had lost some of its swash. A scathing December 21, 1975 review in the *Rocky Mountain News* found that "[t]he restaurant gives off an inescapable aura of catering to two classes of persons—tourists and the tastelessly rich."[131]

Lafitte's rebounded from that printed attack before landing into trouble in 1983 when the property owner, A.H. Cook Company, sued Joe Sperte for $16,000 for unpaid rent.[132] In the wake of the lawsuit, Sperte relocated for a while in Cherry Creek, and eventually the buccaneer quietly left the scene. Sperte's Lafitte's had led the transformation of skid row Larimer Street toward trendy Larimer Square.

Sperte may have boasted that he was the man who brought gourmet to Denver, but the heavyweight champion of twentieth-century haute cuisine was Pierre Wolfe.

BON APPÉTIT

A five-foot-five, relentless tower of self-promotion, Pierre Wolfe's parents died in a Nazi concentration camp while he fought in the Free French Army in North Africa. After the war, Wolfe worked as a steward and assistant chef on the Cunard luxury liners and subsequently studied at *École Hôtelière de Lausanne* in Switzerland. Following the path of previous Frenchmen on the prairie like the Charpiots, Wolfe came to Denver to visit to his sister in 1950. Starting in the Brown Palace kitchen as a night chef, in under a year, Wolfe began his first job as a chef at the Patio in Littleton.

Near the Centennial racecourse, the Patio was easily one of Littleton's, if not the entire Front Range's, swankiest places. Led by a team of African American waiters who previously served on railroad dining cars, the Billy Wilson Trio providing the mellow sounds, and Buzzie the bartender mixing the drinks, the Patio was a hipster's dream in the country. A contemporary photo of Wolfe in gleaming white toque and serving the special of the day to Swedish film star Anita Ekberg underscores the swinging yet surreal image.

When the Patio's owner defaulted on the lease, the landlord gave Wolfe the restaurant's keys. Littleton was too far away from the action for such a dynamo. As the 1960s dawned, Wolfe rented the old Argonaut Hotel coffee shop across from the state capitol and opened the Quorum. The Quorum was

Pierre Wolfe's control over continental dining in Denver was a family thing. Wolfe and his cousin Heinz Gertsle oversaw the renovation of house that became the Normandy. *From Papers of Pierre Wolfe, WH1465, Western History Collection, Denver Public Library.*

Denver's temple of continental refinement during the Kennedy and Johnson years. Anecdotes about the Quorum are numerous. Wolfe denied entry to an improperly attired Marlon Brando; chastened, he returned wearing a jacket. Actress Jane Asher celebrated her twenty-first birthday in April 1967 with her boyfriend, a musician by the name of Paul McCartney. The following captures Wolfe's interpretation of 1960s high-seas haute cuisine.

Casserole Neptune

4 ounces lobster, cooked

2 teaspoons onion, finely chopped

½ cup cream

4 tablespoons all-purpose flour

pinch thyme, salt, and pepper

1 teaspoon grated American cheese

4 ounces shrimp, cooked

2 cups milk

8 teaspoons butter

1 ounce sauterne wine

1 teaspoon grated Parmesan cheese

paprika

Dice cooked seafood in half-inch squares. Simmer onions in milk and cream for 10 minutes. Meanwhile, combine butter with flour in deep saucepan and stir until smooth. Cook for 5 minutes, stirring continuously. The roux must not get brown. Now strain milk and cream into saucepan with butter and flour mixture. Stir until blended. Add wine, thyme, salt, pepper, and half of the quantity of cheeses. Now combine seafood with sauce. Place in casserole. Sprinkle with remainder of cheeses and then sprinkle with paprika. Brown in casserole in a hot oven or under the broiler. Serve with wild or white rice. To arrange a colorful plate, use crabapple for garnish and asparagus for a vegetable.[133]

At the Quorum, salads arrived in an iced cart, and hot food appeared in copper skillets for a regular litany of senators, lobbyists, and other officials who spent their days across Colfax in the state capitol. With true continental *élan*, the proprietor prepared tableside two-pieces of a New York strip steak touched with a stingy coating of Grey Poupon mustard, mushrooms, butter, garlic, shallots, parsley, green onions, Worcestershire sauce, and fresh ground pepper; cooked in corn oil; flamed with cognac; and served with brown sauce. Wolfe claimed that he prepared at least sixty thousand steaks Diana, *à la Pierre* over the decades.

His cooking, presentation, and the rarified clientele made Wolfe the city's most recognizable restaurateur. Even if you never crossed the burgundy carpet to one of the Quorum's purple chairs, Pierre Wolfe was on your TV conducting cooking demonstrations or on the radio as a commercial spokesman. He ran his own restaurant review show and was the local media's go-to gourmet. The pace had slowed down somewhat by April 1990. During the 1970s, the restaurant averaged three hundred customers Friday and Saturday nights and grossed as much as $1.2 million per year. By the time it closed in April 1990, seatings had dropped to an average of 150 customers per night, but Wolfe's restaurant still collected an enviable $600,000 to $700,000 annually.[134]

A few weeks before the last night, and speaking in the third person, Wolfe (like other restaurateurs) employed a theatrical reference: "Every night, the curtain goes up, and Pierre has been on stage. Now, how many people have a chance to orchestrate their own ending?"[135] More than two decades later, he authors the occasional book and still hosts a weekly radio call-in show focusing on the Denver dining scene.

Before the Quorum opened, the Wolfe family capitalized on Lucien Broch's failure to establish a piece of European sophistication on East

The Normandy was East Colfax's finest restaurant when the avenue was gaining a reputation as the "longest, wickedest street in America." *From authors' collection.*

Colfax. Wolfe and his cousin, Heinz Gerstle, purchased the Normandy in 1958 for $8,500 and quickly put the restaurant at the top of Denver's continental dining destinations. Gerstle built a new Normandy nearby at 1515 Madison Street in the early 1970s. Wolfe and his wife, Jean, bought out Gerstle in 1990 and handed the daily operations to their daughter, Karen Hermann. Hermann trained as a chef in France and worked in cities across the United States. Upon returning to Denver, Hermann managed the Normandy and Chez Michelle, a bistro located at the front of the building. Hermann decided to leave the restaurant business, and the Normandy closed in 2000.[136]

Another restaurant with a woman front and center was Tante Louise. Critics and diners recognized Tante Louise as one of the city's dining jewels during the 1970s and 1980s. Owner Corky Douglass featured the following.

Tante Louise's Roasted Five-Spiced Half Duck

DUCK BRINE

1 orange	*1 onion*
10 cloves garlic	*3 ounces sliced ginger*
¼ cup plus 1–2 tablespoons Chinese five-spice powder	*¼ cup soy sauce*
1 gallon water	*½ cup salt*
12 star anise	*1 cup brown sugar*
6 cups ice	*1 four- to six-pound duck*

Bring orange, onion, garlic, ginger, five-spice powder, soy sauce, water, salt, star anise, and brown sugar to a boil and cook for 30 minutes. Remove from heat and add ice. Let ice melt and then refrigerate brine. When cool, immerse whole duck completely in brine 8 to 18 hours. Remove from brine, pat dry, and place duck on a rack in pan in a 325-degree oven for 45 minutes. Remove drippings with baster and continue to roast until meat thermometer reads 175 degrees Fahrenheit in the thickest part of the thigh—about 2.5 hours more. Remove and let it rest for 30 minutes. Then cut into halves and place ducks under a broiler until crispy.[137]

Pierre Wolfe, Heinz Gerstle, Karen Hermann, and Corky Douglass created countless memorable meals. These were for people who wouldn't blink when presented with the bill. A contemporary chain restaurant reached more people and lingers in more memories for reasons different than those created by Pierre Wolfe.

THE ROOSTER STILL CROWS

It is the spring of 2014, and you're driving in your car, flipping through the few hundred or so sports talk stations on the radio dial. At a break from analyzing the Broncos' seventh-round draft pick, a voice deep with nostalgia and dripping with portent asks, "If you remember the train going round and round at the Denver Drumstick—Then You Belong with Us."

What do you call a restaurant that valued hot grease over haute cuisine and served its last fried chicken more than forty years ago but continues to cause Denver residents of a certain age to daydream about their innocent youth? You would call it the Denver Drumstick.

When asked what they missed most about dining in Denver, a typical response from those over the age of forty-five interviewed for this book said that it was the model train chugging along over the heads of diners at the Denver Drumstick. It reveals that childhood memories are stronger than a spectacular meal. Both the Denver Drumstick and the White Spot remain memorable for surroundings more than menu. The Denver Drumstick was Sunday dinner, while the White Spot provided the carbohydrates and coffee for sobering up as Friday night melted into Saturday morning.

Austin Meyers ended the Second World War as a west Texas poultry farmer with a problem. The military was moving out of Texas, and he had a lot of chickens on his hands. War or no war—people still had to eat. So with his chickens, Meyers started a restaurant in Amarillo. A second successful branch in west Texas led Meyers to build an outpost of his fried chicken empire at 6801 West Colfax Avenue in Lakewood in 1955. Within a decade, he had added five more restaurants and closed the original West Colfax address. Meyers reopened with a fifteen-thousand-square-foot palace a few hundred feet to the east in front of the JCRS shopping center. Completed in 1966, the glass and faux stone exterior of the "super deluxe" Drumstick cost $75,000, and the restaurant sat four hundred customers. Promotional material from the time explained why the Drumstick's wings, breasts, and thighs were better than any other restaurant. Its menu explained:

> *Our Farm has justly earned the name of being the largest producer of fine Battery-Fed fryers in this entire section of the country—producing more than 250,000 fryers annually. Our chickens are raised in concrete block buildings and constant temperature is maintained the year around. They never touch the ground. All chickens feed continuously day and night on a special Feed Formula.*[138]

Similar to one of its chickens, Denver Drumstick's "Facts About Our Poultry Farm" wouldn't fly nowadays.

The Drumstick is memorable not so much for its food but for the trappings that went along with it. Parents brought the Denver Drumstick home with a family pack of fried chicken in a cardboard railroad boxcar. Kids were the target audience for the "Drumstick Special," served in a cardboard fire wagon. Or the fried shrimp in a boat-shaped box complete with sail and pennant. Great fun if you were a pre-pubescent Denverite of the 1960s. Not so much when you came home from school one day to find that your mother had thrown out your greasy fire wagon from a couple nights back.

Meyer saved his *pièce de résistance* for those diners who chose to eat in the restaurant. A miniature train ran around the interior of each Denver Drumstick. The JCRS branch boasted six hundred feet of track, with miniature trains moving in opposite directions. The trains clocked an average of thirty thousand miles per year. The motorized distractions took the diner on a panoramic journey through Colorado—through Mesa Verde, Cripple Creek, and a miniature Moffat Tunnel. Meyers explained that the constantly running trains kept "restless youngsters in their chairs while they're eating."[139]

Baby boom–era restaurateurs increasingly sought to please kids—as long as their parents picked up the tab. One of those places remembered more for its location than its cuisine was the Sky Chef restaurant in Stapleton Airport's Terminal Building. Before the landing strip added "International" to its title, many of Denver's children trooped out on their birthdays to

"Where Everybody Eats Chicken and Shrimp." Like the Rockies dominate the view to the west, the Denver Drumstick looms large in the memories of many locals. *Menu Collection, 30001562, Western History Collection, Denver Public Library.*

watch planes land and listen to Tony Muro play "Happy Birthday" on the Steinway grand piano as a server brought out a cake with a sparkler on top. Before Sky Chef flew off into forever, many longtime residents recalled that it was *the* place for a child's birthday in the days before Casa Bonita and Chuck E. Cheese.

Back at the Drumstick, an adult could only watch the train go around and around for so long. Conversation about the Drumstick's menu usually comes around to the gravy and a thick slab of white bread known as Texas toast. Butter was dabbed on both sides of the bread, and then it was placed under a broiler. At the table, this treat was covered with honey. The gravy was a different matter. The yellow, viscous addition inspired two camps: addicts and opponents. Proponents insisted that the gravy lifted up that restaurant newcomer—instant mashed potatoes—to new heights. Here approximates the Drumstick's gravy.

Denver Drumstick Gravy

Take chicken stock from powder, mix with water and set to boil. Once at a boil, reduce heat to low. In a separate pan, mix flour and oil (1:1 ratio) to make a roux. Heat and stir the roux until it starts to turn clear. Estimate 1 cup of roux for 1 gallon of stock. Let the roux sit for a few minutes and then stir into the chicken stock. The mixture will thicken quickly.[140]

The Denver Drumstick fried its last chicken in the early 1970s, but the restaurant's hold on Denver remains. A remodeling of the Drumstick at Lakewood's JCRS into a bingo parlor during the 1980s gave the palace a second life. Bingo went away around the early 2000s, but the exposed bits

Etched in the front door of a long-empty restaurant, the Denver Drumstick's rooster remains at its West Colfax location. *Photo by Kristen Autobee.*

of trim and the shape of the picture windows still indicate to students of Denver restaurant architecture that this was the grandest of all Drumsticks. Perhaps a future archaeological dig will uncover the remains of a model railroad.

"The Savior of Many of Us"

The White Spot went by the catchphrase "Won't you make the White Spot your next stop?" but that was quickly unnecessary for Denver's denizens of the dark. In 1964, the *Denver Post* discovered that the "White Spot Is for Pilgrims of Late, Late Scene." So read the headline above Barry Morrison's August 18 entertainment column. But who were those after-midnight types? "After the dancing girls have wrapped up their costumes and fled into the night...after the musicians have cased their axes and are on the nod...after the grog shops have shuttered their doors." The light they all followed shone from the White Spot.[141]

The White Spot remains Denver's best example of the work of architects Armet and Davis of Los Angeles and their ability to make glass, steel beams, and concrete threaten to take flight. Armet and Davis were the team behind the Southern California architectural style known as "Googie." The Googies of metropolitan Los Angeles were the prototype for Denver's White Spot. Googie reflected the high spirits and moment of change found in the early days of America's space age. The Colorado Café at the southwest corner of West Colfax Avenue and Speer Boulevard and Tom's Diner at 601 East Colfax are two surviving examples of Armet and Davis's work. Not everyone appreciated White Spot's design and atmosphere. In a review of Lakewood's Taylor's Supper Club, a critic from *Cervi's Business Journal* noted that the club's "décor suggests a dimly lit White Spot."[142]

The man in the (white) spot was William F. Clements. Clements grew up in Monte Vista and started his career in his family's bakeries in Denver, Fort Lupton, and Greeley. He opened the first White Spot at 22 South Broadway in 1947. Twenty years later, seven White Spots were grossing $3 million—all based on an average bill totaling $0.80 cents. In 1969, Clements was comfortable enough to tell the *Rocky Mountain News* at the opening of the eighth White Spot that he had made it his business to travel and pick up ideas from all over the country and adapt them to what customers in Denver wanted.[143]

You could start bright at the White Spot even if the day started at two o'clock in the morning. *From* Jefferson Sentinel, *March 31, 1960.*

That same year, the White Spot found itself embroiled with the city's growing hippy community. In August 1969, Bob Warren, manager of the White Spot at 601 East Colfax, refused service to a group of counterculture counter customers, as "the majority of other customers found them objectionable." The hippies' representative shot back that it was "because of our dress, hair and life-style are not prepackaged, homogenized and plastic like their formica food."[144] Ronald Charles, twenty-one, of Littleton asked for $500 damages from the White Spot. The case went all the way to Denver Superior Court judge Charles Bennett, who upheld a lower court ruling permitting restaurants to serve customers at their own discretion except where it involved "a racial situation." In affirming the lower court's decision, Judge Bennett's opinion found that "no one would want to eat dinner in an atmosphere of barefooted, semi-dressed, disheveled, unwashed people, who throw food about at each other and on the floor and general conduct themselves in atmosphere not conductive to comfortable, restful, relaxed eating. Good food, well-prepared, well-served, in good surroundings is the savior of many us."[145]

Tony Clements took over the operation of the White Spots after his father, William, died in 1971. Tony went about closing or selling the restaurants by the mid-1980s. For the next decade and a half, the last White Spot held on at 8th and Broadway. By the Reagan years, on most weekend nights you could see poorly put-together drag queens, substance abusers, and the loud arguing with the profane. If William Clements had been around, he might have asked the hippies to come back for another cup of coffee.

The lights went out at 7:15 a.m. on June 25, 2001. Staff went through the unusual process of locking the doors on this twenty-four-hour, seven-days-a-week Denver landmark. Closing the White Spot brought out many to reminisce to the local media. "If I walked into Denny's like this, I couldn't relax because everybody would be staring or trying to start trouble," Jonathan Allen told the *Denver Post*. Allen's pale skin, red lipstick, and six-inch-high hair probably would have stopped him from finishing his coffee at most suburban Perkins or Village Inn restaurants. The White Spot's misunderstood (but still architecturally and historically important) design did not dissuade property owner Mile High Development from demolishing the building. The 8th and Broadway site stood empty for nearly a decade before a national chain bank rose from the long-empty lot.[146]

Tom's Diner and Colorado Café have kept the locations, mood, and spirit of the old White Spot alive. Every city needs a place like the White Spot. Days before closing, waitress Jennifer Morris pointed to the restaurant's burnt-orange upholstery and summed up why the denizens of the night kept the White Spot alive: "They solve all the world's problems from those chairs."[147]

THE FIVE POINTS FAMILY

As the Quorum, White Spot, and Denver Drumstick served the city's growing suburbs and increasingly downtrodden downtown, Denver's African American neighborhood, Five Points, supported a handful of establishments that would be associated with the community for many decades.

Denver's African American community slowly developed its own popular dining spots, as the downtown restaurants wouldn't always serve people of color. Five Points was home to a number of small mom and pop restaurants in the first half of the twentieth century, but two stand out from the century's latter half: those of "Daddy" Bruce Randolph and Lawrence Pierre.

From every Thanksgiving feed to feeding the Denver Broncos every time they played an away game, Randolph was an ambassador of goodwill for Five Points. Bronco cornerback Louis Wright recalled in the 1980s, "I met him about 10 years ago and at the time he usually would have all the Bronco players over for lunch and dinner and let us eat free…I think more than anything he's just the epitome of what every human being should be like."[148]

Emblazoned on the exterior of Bruce Randolph's restaurant, on his pickup truck's sideboards, and on every bottle of barbecue sauce sold in the city's supermarkets was Bruce Randolph's code for living: "God loves you, so does Daddy Bruce."

The story surrounding Randolph's cooking traces back to his grandmother in Arkansas passing on her secret barbecue recipe to a young Bruce. Randolph was unable to capitalize on this secret for nearly five decades. He lived a life as a barber and shoe shiner before he opened a restaurant in his sixty-eighth year.

After a life packed with giving, community involvement, and smoking meat and ribs, the City of Denver honored "Daddy" Bruce by renaming 34th Avenue—from Stapleton Airport through Five Points to City Park—Bruce Randolph Avenue in 1985. No other Denver chef, cook, or restaurateur had received a similar honor, and by the end of the decade, Randolph was deeply in debt. The city took away his restaurant in 1990 for back taxes, and Randolph died four years later at the age of ninety-four. Daddy Bruce's giving lives on through the Daddy Bruce Legacy Thanksgiving Dinner of turkey and fixings served from 10:00 a.m. until the food is gone. Epworth UMC also hosts the Denver Feed a Family program for families, who receive baskets of turkey, potatoes, green beans, macaroni and cheese, cornbread mix, and cranberries.[149]

Lawrence Pierre also achieved legendary status in Five Points, but he went about it over a longer period and following a more roundabout route through other Denver neighborhoods.

Pierre and Ollie Mae Jackson opened Pierre's BBQ in the late 1940s at 5122 West 1st Avenue, close to Denver's Barnum neighborhood. Barbecue and fried chicken brought customers. Barnum resident Peggy Nelson recalled that when the smoker was going, "You could smell barbecue all over the neighborhood." It was so good that Nelson and her husband-to-be ate there the night before their wedding. By the mid-1950s, Pierre had relocated to 2550 Washington before eventually settling at 2157 Downing in Five Points.[150]

In 1962, Pierre's Supper Club opened as a small restaurant featuring the old standby, fried chicken, joined by a new item, catfish. Pierre told the *Rocky Mountain News* in 1990 that his secret seasoning for catfish came from the Bahamas. Soon his supper club sold seventy-five pounds of catfish each day and marketed spices and other cooking items in local grocery stores. Over time, the supper club became the largest black-owned restaurant/nightclub in Colorado, with a five-thousand-square-foot showroom and disco.[151] From sponsoring the sports talk radio shows of the city's first African American host, Thierry Smith, to following a plan not to finance the business through borrowed money, Pierre believed that his restaurant should be more than just a place for a good meal. "When Pierre's Supper Club started out in 1962, not many businesses would hire black people. We did. We have always treated our employees well…like they owned part of the business. We continued to hire people from the neighborhood and, as a result, the money that we paid in salary was turned over several times before it left the community."[152]

Ethel's House of Soul and M&D Café were also places for diners to come to and from Five Points. The catfish and peach cobbler at M&D's was so addictive that Secretary of Energy (and former Denver mayor) Federico Peña had his staff call for a two-thousand-mile to-go order. From the edge of Cherry Creek to the banks of the Potomac, FedEx was happy to deliver Secretary Peña his soul food fix overnight.

Denver faced the 1970s like a teenager asking for a first job—there were flashes of confidence, but it was still awkward. For the final thirty years of the twentieth century, the city's political and business leaders often wondered how the city would earn a piece of the national spotlight. Concurrently, the city's mom and pop places found themselves under attack by the restaurant "industry." This industry was run by marketers basing decisions on outside consultants from both coasts and test kitchens. No matter. Times were good, and Denver found itself as an industry destination.

CHAPTER 5

"Every Day the Curtain Goes Up"

DENVER IN SEARCH OF ITS OWN TUNE, 1970–1990

O ften atmosphere superseded location—and many times at the cost of an enjoyable dining experience—as the goal of the successful restaurateur by the early 1970s. This was the era of the theme restaurant nationwide, and despite its proximity to the Rocky Mountains, Denver could not hide from this wave of outlandishness. During the decade, one could go ducal England (the Piccadilly), coastal New England (Fisherman's Cove), a World War I trench and aerodrome (94th Aero Squadron), visit a Dutch windmill (the Hungry Dutchman), or survive a United Nations of fried delights (the Yum Yum Tree). This was the era of Denver restaurants that were owned by corporations or interests living elsewhere. They had money for advertising, promotion, and, most importantly, national inescapability. Every diner knew the menus of most of Denver's restaurants by heart: salad for starters with entrées of steak, prime rib, or lobster. However, as the '70s hit its stride, other tastes offered a change.

The nation's culinary pendulum had swung back to the importance of well-prepared food by the late 1980s, but the previous decade remains memorable for the number of establishments that valued the experience over the meal. Near the end of this arbitrary two-decade bracket, Denver briefly garnered recognition for a single chef and his restaurant.

The home side was well represented with a new generation of Denver restaurateurs. Leading this group was Tom Wilscam and Leo Goto. Frank Pourdad and Jimmy Schmidt joined them. Each used various elements of entertainment, elegance, and individuality against an encroaching march of dining Disneylands.

ALWAYS ON THE OFFENSIVE

"I never enjoyed bowing and scraping waiters."

First known as the "Other Guard" from his days on the University of Colorado football team's offensive line, Tom Wilscam parlayed luck and the right attitude to alter the city's dining habits. Wilscam's methods democratized dining and establishing restaurants beyond the banks of Cherry Creek to the four corners of the burgeoning metropolitan area. He was Denver's Horatio Alger in the age of Abbie Hoffman. Both Denver dailies followed the successes of first the Hungry Farmer, then the Hungry Dutchman, then the Broker, and then his other ventures in other parts of the country. He played for big stakes, and he eventually found that running a restaurant wasn't fun if it wasn't hands on.

Wilscam had a three-step philosophy to creating a successful restaurant that he has carried through the past fifty years and myriad restaurants: first, food; second, atmosphere; and third, service.

Wilscam admitted that his notoriety led to his first restaurant management job. He asked his basketball, track, and football buddies (two all-Americans and an Olympic medalist) from the University of Colorado to wait tables. Wilscam recalled, "The food wasn't very good…and the service was worse."[153]

Following the lure of the dining room, Wilscam moved on to the Alpine Village Inn at 1150 South Colorado Boulevard in Denver. Surrounded by Old Regiment steins, kerosene lamps, and waitress *frauleins* in Bavarian peasant costumes serving homemade soup made from scratch with bone stock and fresh vegetables. The main courses included zarter kapaun (roast caponette), schnitzel, and sauerbraten.[154] He admitted that that owner Ray Danbaugh taught him all he later adapted and refined in his subsequent ventures. After a few years, Wilscam was ready to call his own plays.

The *Denver Post*'s Barry Morrison captured the essence of the theme restaurant dining in his October 13, 1964 review of Wilscam's Hungry Farmer: "The Hungry Farmer turned out to be a place for seeing as much as dining." After entering the farmhouse, a diner would come upon the Farmer's bag of tricks: "In the corner stands a huge, high still. It's a copper gleaming dolly…it isn't a hallucination, but for real, when the still begins emitting a hissing sound and begins to shake. It does this every 15 minutes or so."[155]

Wilscam loved the theatrics of dining: "Every day the curtain goes up. I'll admit that I'm kind of a showman."[156] There was talk in the Denver papers of Wilscam franchising in twenty-nine other cities. The Farmer was Denver dining's smash hit of the mid-1960s. Wilscam took his next show out of town—way out of town—to Interstate 25 and Arapahoe Road. Before the

In the 1960s, Denver restaurateur Tom Wilscam brought fun to dining at the Hungry Farmer and, later, the Hungry Dutchman. *From authors' collection.*

Holland on the prairie. The Hungry Dutchman was an I-25 landmark in the days before the Denver Tech Center. *From authors' collection.*

Wilscam reached his apex as a restaurateur with the Broker. The Broker started in the basement of an old bank and eventually opened branches throughout Denver. *From authors' collection.*

Hungry Dutchman opened in 1966, Wilscam had to build a road to reach the lone Dutch windmill on the prairie. The differences between the Farmer and the Dutchman were the cut of servers' uniforms and names of entrées and drinks. Wilscam enjoyed subsequent success with the Broker, PTI, and Wilscam's on 17th and Arapahoe Street.

FROM TIKIS TO TASTE

A son of Japanese Americans who spent the war in an internment camp, Leo Goto rose from dishwasher to manage Denver's Outrigger. The Trader Vic's conglomerate owned the Outrigger located in Cosmopolitan Hotel on Broadway. Goto came up fast in the organization and eventually opened branches of Trader Vic's in Portland, Houston, and London. In 1968, he left Trader's Vic's to open Leo's Place on the southeast corner of Broadway and 16th Street in downtown Denver. A former coffee shop, he retrofitted the place with furnishings from old Denver mansions, playing heavily on a "Leo the Lion" theme. Goto's friend and owner of The Fort, Sam Arnold, noted, "The wash bowl in the ladies room is a landmark of antique decorative porcelain." Another reviewer gushed that "the immaculately clean linen and the quiet, gracious service [are] a welcome relief from paper placemats and fatuous cheer dished out in so many establishments."[157]

The menu at Leo's Place reflected Goto's experience from Trader Vic's with an acknowledgement of newer ingredients and recipes: "Artichoke hearts, ceviche, Chinese barbecued pork, crepes stuffed with tiny bay shrimp…or crab…or mushrooms, etc."[158] Goto was aware of the slowly developing sophistication of Denver's better-off diners, and he was there to lead them on.

As a shrewd marketer, Goto kept other menu items influenced by the faux Polynesia of Trader Vic's. For $7.95, one variation of the "Western Luau" opened with "tempura tidbits served with hot, hot mustard and regular ketchup" and salad, teriyaki steak, pineapple pork, Chinese peas, and white chestnuts. This trip to the islands concluded with an "Aspen Snowball"—ice cream with a meringue base and chocolate syrup and covered with coconut.[159]

In 1980, urban renewal forced Goto to leave downtown to start the Wellshire Inn at 3333 South Colorado Boulevard and near the city-owned Wellshire Golf Course. Not everything went smoothly. A *Rocky Mountain News* exposé found that the Wellshire and its partners—Goto, lawyer Lawrence Alter, and real estate developer Howard Torgove—had avoided making annual payments of $8,800 for utilities to the city. A meal at the Wellshire was so serious that Denver's mayor for life, William McNichols, stepped in to resolve the issue and quickly. After the city settled with the trio, McNichols said that he was "satisfied with the agreement and I'm not so mad I won't eat out there."[160] The Wellshire's owners were poor winners. The agreement would cost Denver taxpayers several thousand dollars over the next fifteen years, but everybody should be happy because "Denver has a first-class restaurant that wouldn't otherwise exist."[161]

Wilscam and Goto were Denver's homegrown restaurateurs-showmen during the 1960s to the 1980s. They faced outside concepts, themes, and outright outlandishness from the national restaurant industry. A cockeyed blend of history, cultural stereotypes, and popular perceptions formed the marketing plans for far too many attempts to launch successful restaurants.

OFF TUNE

Food historians and connoisseurs of the commonplace Jane and Michael Stern make the case that the theme restaurant extends back to the Moorish- and rococo-themed restaurants of Depression-era Hollywood. One place in Tinseltown called the Pirate's Den featured a floorshow culminating in mock floggings. If one wants to stretch the concept of theme restaurants to its breaking point, Denver's earliest example could be the Old Dutch Mill at 1545 Champa. Launched by Theron C. Bennett in 1910, the Mill was initially a cabaret, but with the impending doom brought by strict state laws against alcohol, the Mill transformed into a cafeteria in 1915. A windmill in the corner looked down on waitresses in Dutch costumers with wide wing caps. One patron, Mildred Crysler, recalled, "There was a ramp running from the rear of the balcony to the street floor, and chorus girls danced down it while singing popular songs. The only night I attended they presented 'Only a Rose' and ended by throwing long-stemmed American Beauty roses over the balcony to the men seated below."[162]

An economic depression, a world war, and a desire to maintain the status quo put the lid on places like the Old Dutch Mill for the next few decades. This changed as the postwar baby boom was just beginning to pop. Larger numbers of middle-class parents with children wanted a good time with their meal. Both the Yum Yum Tree and the 94th Aero Squadron started elsewhere (Arizona and California, respectively), but they were soon favorites of many Denver families. It didn't matter that the two restaurants both featured rather ordinary food.

The roots of the Yum Yum Tree reached to Phoenix, Arizona, where a sister restaurant, the Pepper Tree, established the idea of a "multi-culti" cafeteria in the early 1960s. However, after its arrival later in the decade, it didn't take long for Denverites to become Tree huggers. Why, with Denver's very own Blinky the Clown in your commercials, few Denver couples were strong enough to resist their children begging to visit.[163]

The Yum Yum Tree had it all: 302 different dishes! Four dining rooms! Seating for up to six hundred people! Cherry Creek North and South Colorado Boulevard had never seen anything like it. The names of the separate restaurants are burned into the minds of many Denverites over fifty: Adam's Rib (hamburgers and ribs), Apple Annie's confectionaries, Fat Eddie's (steaks and chops), Fellini's (Italian), Hoffbrauhaus (German), Poncho's Patio (Mexican), and Tommy Wong's (Chinese).

No time to smoke, must order an enchilada with egg foo young. All cultures' cuisines were on one buffet line at the Yum Yum Tree. *From authors' collection.*

Denver writer Sally Stitch penned a charming recollection of the Yum Yum Tree from her days as a student at the University of Denver in the late 1960s. She recalled, "Goofy as it sounds now, it was adventuresome dining and it was affordable."[164] Stitch's fondness for the Yum Yum Tree manifested itself decades later in high school and college graduation parties for her son and daughter. The Yum Yum Tree was long gone by the time the honorees were graduates, but Stitch's menu for the occasion reads like a 1960s Denver's version of a Valhalla banquet: Tommy Wong's mini egg rolls, the Denver Drumstick's fried chicken drummettes with Texas toast, and Round the Corner's mini Caesar burgers. Blinky the Clown was the only one missing from the guest list.

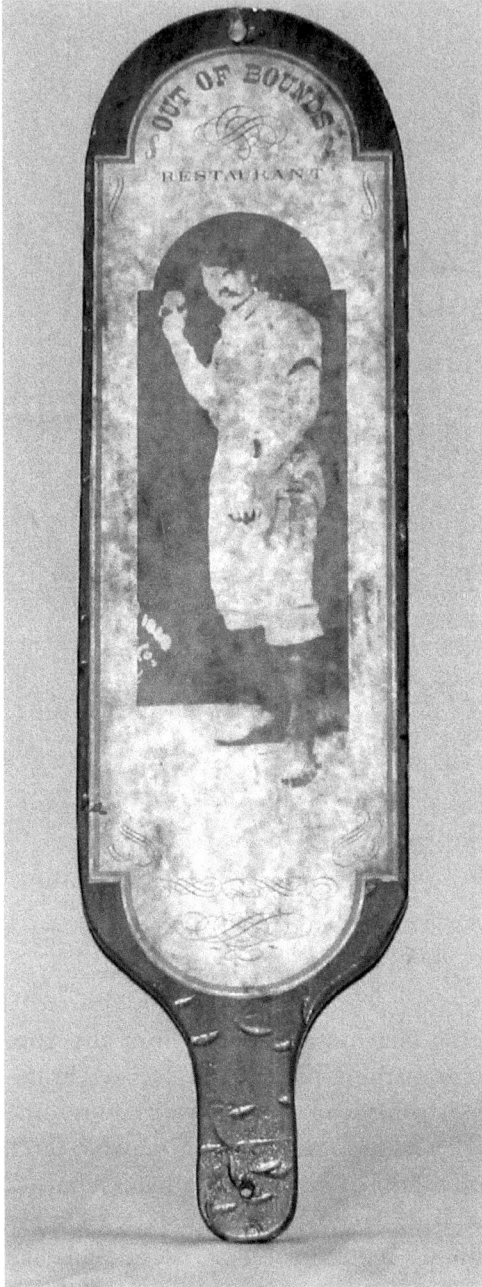

Knute Rockne and Barney Oldfield unwittingly lent their names to the steak-heavy menu of the sports-themed Out of Bounds in Aurora. *From authors' collection.*

The 94th Aero Squadron had the strangest of come-ons. Brought to you by Specialty Restaurants Corporation of Anaheim in 1974 (which also gave Denver Baby Doe's, the Chili Pepper, and Brittany Hill), Specialty Restaurants knew that people would want to watch planes take off, listen to the control tower, and hunker down in a stylized re-creation of a World War I trench. Well, maybe ten-year-old boys would. Biplanes, machine gun nests, sandbags, and a glass wall faced Stapleton Airport's runway. The only things missing were barbed wire and phosgene gas. In Denver, it worked for a while, but the war on good taste finally came to an ironic end in 1990 when an electrical fire gutted the building. Specialty Restaurants is no longer in the Denver market, but its last squadron is still in operation next to the airport in Van Nuys, California.[165]

Representatives of national chains based on a theme (Victoria Station) and a handful of local attempts to merge atmosphere with dinner (the Library and Out of Bounds, to name a pair) kept diners in sizzling steaks and Green Goddess dressing on their salads for most of the decade. Owner Bud Hawkins ran the Library at

800 South Colorado Boulevard. The gimmick beyond the prime rib, lobster, and salad was a roomful of books—most purchased from Goodwill or the Salvation Army. Another forgotten candidate in the style-over-substance category was Aurora's Out of Bounds. Based on a perception of nineteenth-century sporting life, the Out of Bounds steaks, prime rib, and chicken breasts marinated in wine, soy sauce, and sweet vermouth didn't help the restaurant survive past the mid-1970s.[166]

Jane and Michael Stern observed that theme restaurants have survived, and all live flamboyantly in Las Vegas. The celebrity chef eateries "reflect the theme restaurant concept, the theme in these cases being fine dining, with a menu and ambience meant to replicate the original experience that is somewhere else."[167]

Tom Wilscam disagreed slightly: "You still have theme restaurants—it's just changed. Nearly every place today has a theme. Maggiano's—there's a theme. Even Le Central [a chateau anchored at the corner of 9th and Lincoln for the past thirty years]. If you think about it, that's a theme restaurant. These places help make dining out an occasion." For many diners, bread will always need a circus as an accompaniment.[168]

That's All You're Gonna Get—Steak, Salad, and a Potato

Holly Arnold Kinney recalled her Denver childhood as a time of some adventure. As an adult working in the restaurant business, "I'd meet with people from the East Coast and they would say, 'Denver—that's all steaks' and I'd say we have fabulous sashimi at the Fuji En. Chinese, Thai…are you kidding me?"[169]

Despite Ms. Kinney's strident defense, there was some truth in that stereotype. Richard Pinhorn's foundation for the success of The Manhattan in the 1890s was local dining's brown cloud remaining over the city for most of the twentieth century. Not that Denver was recognized nationally as a great steak city like Kansas City, but the Mile High City sure liked its meat.

Denver was growing beyond its traditional boundaries by the early 1960s. The Tally Ho was waaaaay out in the suburbs at the corner of Wadsworth and Alameda after it opened in 1962. Where cattle until only recently had chomped on grass, Billy Wilson and his partner, Joel Barron, built a supper club. Wilson had been part of the exodus, along with Pierre Wolfe from the Patio in Littleton.

The Tally Ho's signage facing the intersection matched the mountains—forty-two feet high and designed like a large lamppost that could be seen two miles away. In those days, Wadsworth and Alameda had no other signs to compete. Once inside the building's shake shingled roof and brick exterior, hosts Billy Wilson and Joel Barron would lead you past the fireside lounge, a section of shuttered booths for an intimate date, to your table in a dining room that sat two hundred people. On the menu, the gold, silver, and bronze medal winners of 1960s dining—prime rib, lobster tail, and steak—were all there.[170]

By the early '70s, the Tally Ho had a rival down Wadsworth. The Jefferson 440 at 440 Wadsworth in Lakewood specialized in cocktails (Manhattans, naturally), small appetizer plates of spaghetti, and main courses featuring that holy trinity of prime rib, steak, and lobster. Opened in 1971, the 440's interior was dark, with sawn cedar, redwood posts, and deep carpet with big red wingback leather chairs surrounding tables of white oak. A 1973 review from the local paper, the *Jefferson Sentinel*, makes for a fascinating read on the restaurant, the times, and the reviewer's priorities: "Management is to be commended for the training and the costuming for the young ladies. All appear in short skirts and the big majority have nice legs (which had nothing to do with our evaluation of services). So much for the calves. On to the steers."

Once the New York steak (for $5.75) and the highest-priced item on the menu, twin lobster tails (at a whopping $6.95), were dispatched, the reviewer offered the highest praise that every suburban restaurant sought: "I thought the 440's quality, cuisine and service puts it in the Cherry Creek and So. Colorado Blvd. class."[171]

There's one tragic shadow over the memory of Jefferson 440. In June 1984, Denver talk show host Alan Berg had his last meal at the 440 before he was ambushed by a white supremacist cowering in the bushes outside his house. The 440 lasted until the 1990s, when a Walmart muscled its way onto the address.

Mixed Grill

It may have been a reflection in time, but it is interesting to notice the similarities of what Denver's diners ate a century apart. The usual menus of 1870 and 1970 mirror each other—filled with broiled steaks and seafood weary from the journey from ocean to the high country. Meat on the hoof was just a given, and you could find a charbroiled treasure anywhere from the Golden Ox to the Cork 'n' Cleaver down to the many Mr. Steak's strategically located in every metro Denver suburb. If it was your birthday, you could eat free at Mr. Steak. You just had to remember to come up with an ID when the bill arrived.

Descended from Lande's, the Golden Ox was set up initially on East Colfax in 1965 by way of the Kansas City stockyards. The Cork 'n' Cleaver opened in 1967 at 4042 East Virginia after the first C 'n' C opened in Scottsdale, Arizona, two years previous. Owner Peter Greene boasted, "We serve only booze." This was the era later romanticized through the *Mad Men* TV series—a half-remembered fantasy of ashtrays on every office desk and three-martini lunches. The menu was etched on cleavers, the wine list was printed on the label of a champagne bottle, and drinking glasses were cut wine bottles. The menu was as standard as a skinny tie and a charcoal-gray suit: a self-serve salad bar and lots of beef recently on the hoof.[172]

Same at Mister G's at 3875 Cherry Creek Drive, with its "Mediterranean-Monterrey décor" and its open charcoal hearth. The Scotch 'n' Sirloin at 12th and Grant also employed an open hearth to broil steaks. Denver had gone back to its medium to well-done roots, as every cut, from T-bone to prime rib, held a place of honor on most menus. The plethora of seafood restaurants from the early 1970s remains intriguing. A century earlier,

Roosters, Bulls, and Camels urged Denverites to have cocktails at Lande's at 3130 East Colfax. A favorite during the 1950s, Lande's became the Golden Ox in the 1961. *From authors' collection.*

oysters were in, but by 1970, they were out, thanks to the closure of New York Harbor's oyster beds. Jet planes and a municipal airstrip ultimately upgraded to Stapleton International Airport, however, meant that lobsters quietly snoozing off the coast of Maine wound up at the Boston Half Shell, Fisherman's Cove, or the fish-y equivalent of Mr. Steak, the Zuider Zee. In the late summer of 1969, the Zuider Zee took up residence in Tom Wilscam's Hungry Dutchman. Started in Colorado Springs, the ZZ (as it was sometimes known) eventually added a second restaurant in the recently completed Cinderella City mall in Englewood. Beginning with a cocktail like the Zuider Spider or the Aruba Swing, the menu ran the briny gamut from gumbo soup to lobster in various forms to frog legs. No bread to start the menu—only hush puppies.[173]

COD OR HADDOCK?

At the same time that steak and prime rib were dominating nearly every menu, the tide was creeping closer to Denver. An American perception of the "Swinging London" of the 1960s caught on in Denver's restaurant scene about five years after the nation first met the Beatles and Mary Quant. National chains like H. Salt Fish and Chips and Arthur Treacher's sprang up to feed commuters and families traveling the ever-lengthening thoroughfares like Wadsworth Boulevard in Lakewood and Washington Street in Thornton. Beyond the clumsy attempt to cash in on all things British, many fish-and-chip fast-food places were among the first to make the claim that eating fish was much healthier than hamburgers. Yes, of course, if you overlooked the grease, the batter, the calories, and the "forgetfulness" of some shop owners to change the grease in the fryers every so often.

Perhaps the best "chippie" from that era is the long-forgotten Sidney's Fish and Chips at 312 East Colfax. In the shadow of the state capitol's golden dome, Sid's started as Prince Charlie's Fish and Chips in the early '70s. Beyond the faux Tudor décor, Sid had a way with a fryer. His menu contained the only memorable "after" (or desert) found among all the other cod and potatoes at all the other Denver fish and chip shops. Sid's took a half-inch ring of pineapple or apple, dipped it in batter, fried it, and then dusted the top with confectioners' sugar. The heat of the batter with the sweetness of the fruit is the Proustian moment from this era.[174]

The King Finds His Sandwich

There is a story that has taken on a mythic position in the city's dining history. In 1976, a jumpsuited Elvis Presley followed his friends on the Denver police force to the Colorado Mine Company in Glendale. There the King found a meal he was fit for: the Fool's Gold Loaf. Owned by Buck and Cindy Scott, the Colorado Mine Company was a place unique to the 1970s—a four-hundred-seat restaurant serving two thousand dinners per night. It idealized a Colorado mining past filled with the likes of Horace and Baby Doe Tabor—a place where picks and shovels were the implements of get-rich-quick transformations. Its clientele was a cross between riding-high oil men and tight-lipped lawyers looking to mix with passing-through-town celebrities like Rod Stewart and Telly Savalas. Denver policemen and their opposite numbers in the city's organized crime family, the Smaldones, all patronized the Colorado Mine Company. Scotts welcomed this crowd every night and lived by the motto "Give 'em More."[175]

Nick Andurlakis is one man who saw it all from the kitchen and lived to tell the tale. From the relative peace provided by the passage of time, Andurlakis and his wife, Kathleen, opened their own diner in Golden in the 1980s. On a quiet Monday afternoon in 2014, Andurlakis recalled an annual staff review of the Mine Company's menu forty years earlier. Staff agreed that there weren't enough items aimed at those below the drinking age. Andurlakis commented that a pair of bacon strips topped each salad. That required frying two to three hundred pounds of bacon every night. Recognizing a potential customer base, and with extra bacon to unload, Andurlakis and the gang in the kitchen took one loaf of French bread, one pound of bacon, one jar of peanut butter, and one jar of blueberry preserves. The sandwich maker took a third of the loaf of bread, cut it into thirds lengthwise, and layered it with one pound of peanut butter, one pound of preserves, and one pound of bacon. The customer with the death wish is awed by what is put in front of him or her—four pounds of sandwich served on a miner's pan.

Most of the Mine Company's patrons viewed the sandwich with trepidation until Elvis Presley and his entourage visited Denver in 1976. Andurlakis heard of Presley's love of peanut butter and bacon. He met the King in Mine Company's kitchen after a show with the come-on: "I know you like bacon." Elvis really wanted a hamburger that night, and he got it, too.

The word spread fast around Denver. The Scotts went from serving a few Fool's Gold sandwiches in a week to two hundred per day. The restaurant

You never get away from your raisin'. The sandwich that Elvis Presley flew across country to eat: the Fool's Gold. *Photo by Robert Autobee.*

hired an extra body in the afternoons to come in and make Fool's Golds just to keep up with the anticipated demand that night.

A few months passed. You are Elvis Presley, and after you conquer the world and think about what you've accomplished, you sit around with your boys at Graceland, and it hits you: you gotta get another Fool's Gold sandwich out in Denver. It happened on his daughter Lisa Marie's eighth birthday. So they hop his private jet, the *Lisa Marie*, in Memphis and land at Stapleton Airport a few hours later. Andurlakis had the honor of delivering twenty-two Fool's Gold sandwiches on a platter out to the jet. Two and a half hours later and satiated, Elvis, Lisa Marie, and the rest of the birthday well-wishers headed back to Memphis.[176]

Andurlakis still has a "slimmed down" Fool's Gold on the menu at his place in Golden—meaning there isn't a pound of each ingredient on the plate. Recently, Andurlakis shipped 650 Fool's Gold sandwiches for an Elvis fan club festival at Graceland.

And from such stories, legends are made.

WE DIDN'T RUN FOR THE BORDER—WE WERE ALREADY THERE

The 1960s in Denver, like the rest of the country, saw the Americanization of Mexican food. Because the cuisine was relatively simple to make, burritos, tacos, and tostadas were cranked out in various degrees of authenticity and deliciousness by a mom and pop in Arvada, Littleton, or Larimer Street. Or they were devised and planned into a concept in a corporate boardroom time zones away.

Over the past fifty years, some have celebrated Denver for its own take on Mexican. A reporter for the *LA Weekly* blog site asked the syndicated columnist Gustavo Arellano for an example of "a Mexican food some would consider phony." He shot back, "Denver has some of the weirdest Mexican food in the country. Take the hamburger patty inside a burrito smothered in orange chile. Or the chile relleno wrapped in a wonton. When I first went to Denver, I said, 'This isn't Mexican food!' But over the years I've realized it is an authentic Mexican food tradition."[177]

A renovated Catholic church, the dark interior of the Original Mexican Café on Osage lingers in the memory as a place where Dracula may have enjoyed a burrito. *From Tom Noel Photo Collection, Auraria Library, AUR-515.*

From burritos and tamales out of a cooler to orange-colored green chili to wonton rellenos, Denver has been a melting pot adapting elements of the new country and the old, sprinkled with a little of the individual cook's imagination. During the tour for his book *Taco USA: How Mexican Food Conquered America*, Arellano pledged his allegiance to "Den-Mex" and its signature dish, the Mexican Hamburger, proclaiming it the best Mexican meal in the United States: "This is a dish as Mexican as the Templo Mayor, as American as the Washington Monument, as Chicano as George Lopez."[178]

Out of cultural shape-shifting came the Mexican Hamburger—a patty smothered with beans, wrapped in a tortilla, and covered with green chili the color of a Denver Bronco's uniform—which got its start at Joe's Buffet at 753 Santa Fe Drive. It now is a menu centerpiece of another local legend, Chubby's. The story goes that one of Joe's servers, Linda (her last name is sadly lost), invented the Mexican Hamburger. Chubby's adapted the recipe after Joe's closed its doors.

Sadly, many times family, co-workers, and acquaintances from Southern California conclude their Denver Mexican meals with shouts of "fraudulent" and "not authentic." Beginning with El Nuevo Chapultepec on Larimer in the 1920s and through the century with Casa Mayan, Casa de Manuel, and the Original Mexican Café, and despite odd mutations like Jose O'Shea's and Casa Bonita, Denver's vision of Mexican food is one of the things locals love the most about their hometown. Spend anytime east of the Mississippi, and you will understand why. All the Mexican restaurants along Federal Boulevard, East Colfax in Aurora, and West Alameda through Denver and Lakewood remain anchors of their neighborhoods. They aren't going anywhere.

SPICY AND SWEET

When President Richard Nixon visited China in 1972, Zhou Enlai, the Chinese premier, gave an impressive dinner. Americans got an idea of what the other side of the globe ate. Satellite images of Cronkite, Chancellor, and Walters described a banquet menu of cold sliced roast duck with pineapple, Sichuan bamboo shoot and egg white soup, and braised chicken with coconut. The thaw in U.S.-Chinese relations opened the door for spicier Szechuan dishes. Thousands of miles from mainland China, in Lakewood, the Golden Dragon was one of the metro area's first Szechuan restaurants. A block south of the Westland Shopping Center and close to a Hugh M. Woods hardware store, you had to concentrate to find the Golden Dragon. Opened by James Chang in September 1973, the Dragon eventually abandoned its Lakewood lair for the greener pastures of the Denver Tech Center to become the Dragon Palace. It did leave behind a memorable dessert—fruity and crispy, like hard candy but with a hot exterior and a cool, soft center.

Honey Crisp Bananas or Apples (aka Spun Bananas or Apples Dessert)

1½ cups oil (1 cup for frying and ½ cup for syrup mixture)

1 cup sugar

1 egg

1 tablespoon cornstarch

3 cups flour

2 tablespoons black sesame seeds

2 cups water

4 cups of fresh fruit (bananas or apples), sliced into bite-sized chunks

plate brushed with cold oil

bowl of ice water

In a frying pan, heat ½ cup oil and add sugar. Turn burner to low heat and stir continuously until a thin syrup forms. Keep on very low heat and continue to stir. In a second frying pan, heat 1 cup of oil. In a bowl, beat the egg and add the cornstarch, flour, sesame seeds, and water to make a batter—not too thin. Dunk fruit in the batter to coat. Then deep-fry fruit in hot oil until golden. Remove fruit and quickly drain off oil. Dip fried bananas into syrup mixture, drop hot into ice water so syrup hardens; serve immediately on a plate brushed with cold oil to prevent sticking.[179]

MON PETIT: TOO MUCH FOR ITS TIME

Out of this age of manufactured atmosphere, there remains a gradually dimming memory of an unlikely island of refinement and haute cuisine in (of all places) Wheat Ridge. Utilizing an early twentieth-century Edwardian home along West 38ᵗʰ Avenue, Feredioun "Frank" Pourdad created Mon Petit. As continental as Pierre Wolfe but as different as the Rattlesnake Club would be a decade later, Pourdad was completely at odds with restaurants that made the mortgage each month on gimmicks.

Frank Pourdad started Mon Petit in 1975 in the haute cuisine hinterlands west of Federal Boulevard. Pourdad was that rare combination of back-of-the-house general and front-of-the-house charmer. Many a lady removing a cigarette from her handbag would gaze up as Pourdad magically appeared with a lighter and a dignified bow. In the late 1970s, Mon Petit featured the Indonesian-Dutch specialty *rijsttafel*. It is a guarantee that, forty years later, very few places in Denver can spell *rijsttafel*, let alone serve it.

Mon Petit—Ton Polémique. Not everybody lost their hearts to Pourdad's rack of lamb, chateaubriand, and *scampi buongusto*. A November 1976 *Denver Magazine* review accused the restaurant of "Denveritis": "This condition is a failing not only of Mon Petit but of many restaurants that try too hard to be what they think is sophisticated or French or worldly. Some few can carry the act off, but most forget that a truly fine restaurant makes diners feel relaxed and pampered rather than self-conscious and uncomfortable."

By 1985, the chateau in Wheat Ridge had become too safe for Pourdad. In August of that year, he took a gamble on an "easy-listening disco/bistro" in the refurbished Tivoli Brewery. Neighbors with the Rattlesnake Club, Club Tivoli drew some bemused reaction from visitors.

A telling August 1986 *Denver Magazine* profile on restaurant critics indicates the demons in Pourdad's character. In retrospect, he tempted karma with remarks about reviewers that are both hysterical and chilling. In the restaurant business, the truth is somewhere between the critic's keyboard the owner's ad copy. He struck out against the *Denver Post*'s critic for complaining in print that his duck was not crisp: "It's cooked in a crock. It says so on the menu. How the hell you gonna have crispy skin when something's cooked in a crock? If I would see the man, I would spit in his face. Why doesn't he write about Furr's Cafeteria, where they serve you cottage cheese with a cherry on top?"[180]

Unfortunately, Pourdad didn't have time to bask in the controversy. On the night of August 6, 1986, when that particular *Denver Magazine* had been in the racks for a few days, Pourdad's Maserati crashed going the wrong way on a street downtown.

THE UNION OF THE SNAKE

Fine dining in an establishment named for a reptile brought Denver dining its most glorious moment of national gastronomic notoriety. In December 1985, the Rattlesnake Club opened. Over the next six months, reviewers from the *New York* and *Los Angeles Times*, as well as gourmets and gourmands from across the nation, found themselves on the top floor of the recently refurbished Tivoli Brewing plant. They fell prey to paillard of buffalo with artichokes and tomato butter, duck hash with black beans and peppers, and desserts like white chocolate ravioli. One day in early 1986, a *Denver Post* reporter found part owner and head chef Jimmy Schmidt improvising in the kitchen:

> *Like a jazz musician who plays notes in front of audiences that even he has never heard before, Schmidt concocts a dozen recipes daily, without any noticeable tension. On this day, he was preparing lobster-and-scallop ravioli; swordfish with grapefruit and ginger; roast rack of veal, sliced off the bone for easy eating, with chanterelles, green peppercorns, Szechwan peppers and a splash white and cream, and venison with red wine, raisins, almonds and brandy, braised chestnuts and fennel. All 30 creations on the menu were his own.*[181]

The Rattlesnake struck Denver like a viper. The old brewery's brick had been air-blasted and shellacked. A color palette of coral contrasted with green-gray "as an unequalled blend of old and new." There was the Roche-Bobois sofa in the grill area, the Georg Jensen silver, and the finest wine cellar the city had ever seen, with an emphasis on American vintners like Schramsberg from Napa. Critics declared that "new American cuisine [has] finally come of age." Heady stuff for a town where, a few years later, a local television station put the opening of the first Macaroni Grill in Cherry Creek on before the weather report.[182]

In May 2014, Schmidt discussed his lifelong interest in understanding how and why things worked. Born in Illinois, he initially worked as a race car mechanic. He subsequently studied electrical engineering at university before taking required language credits in France. Schmidt soon found himself under the spell of two notable Gallic charms: food and wine. His curiosity turned from manifolds and motor oil to emulsifications and butter. After a stint with Madeline Kamman, he moved on to the London Chop House, the "21 Club of Detroit," as Schmidt described it. Down on its luck, the Chop House's fortunes rose with Schmidt in the kitchen. By the mid-1980s, "It was time to do my own thing," he recalled. "Denver had a vibrant dining scene more cosmopolitan, more worldly than most people expected."[183]

He recalled what it was like starting a new venture in a new town: "Needed a name that reflected synergy. We wanted to fit the area, so 'Rattlesnake' worked. Some were confused about 'Club.' We were inclusive, not exclusive. Using 'Club' in the name of the restaurant meant that everybody could join."

Joined by partners Michael McCarty and Bevans Branham, Schmidt brought along his crew from the Detroit Chop House to the Tivoli Brewery. The abandoned Tivoli was one of the last landmarks of the old Auraria neighborhood in the process of transformation by the expansion of two colleges and a university. The restaurant's original layout was a rabbit's warren. The kitchen was the width of a fire escape. Eventually, the Rattlesnake Club added two more kitchens, and to access these kitchens, Schmidt and his team took one of three elevators or eighteen sets of stairs. "Never been in better shape in my life from running," Schmidt reflected.

Schmidt was of the first generation of American chefs since the 1880s who stressed locality in their preparation and ingredients. The Rattlesnake Club was certainly the first modern Denver restaurant of · any note that emphasized Colorado lamb and prime beef and put blue and yellow corn through various interpretations. Schmidt took it even further and used heirloom tomatoes from the Seed Savers Exchange, as well as locally grown basil. Ever the scientist in search of a new flavor, Schmidt and his staff blended salts and fermented vinegars.

Experimenting in silence, Schmidt admitted that he has always run a quiet kitchen: "Run silent, run deep. I'm the only one talking. What I try to teach cooks is sight, feel and, if you are really a good chef, hearing. Especially a sauté cook. The stove's doing all the talking. Hear when moisture is issuing, and it is going on medium." Looking back almost thirty years, Schmidt's reaction to an avalanche of positive impressions to his time in Denver was very "aw shucks": "It was great. I was honored. It was overwhelming how they loved the food."[184]

Looking back, both Jimmy Schmidt and John Lehndorff recalled that in the 1980s, visitors from New York and other points east would fly into Denver, head up to Aspen or Vail, and *then* have something to eat. The Rattlesnake Club created a pit stop for out-of-town high rollers.[185]

Schmidt wasn't the only chef to garner kudos from elsewhere. A 1987 *New York Times* feature on how to spend forty-eight hours in Denver complimented restaurateurs for their rack of lamb encrusted in herbs (Cliff Young's) and warm goat cheese salad with pecans (Strings). The late '80s saw the beginning for these two Denver restaurants and other places as they established 17th Avenue as the upscale successor to Larimer Street.[186]

BOB WAS TOO EARLY

In December 1985, *Westword* food critic Max Stuart raved about a "fast-food restaurant" that should be remembered as a harbinger of two trends that still dominate the national dining scene into the twenty-first century. In an old Mr. Steak at 1007 East Colfax, the Brick Oven Beanery (or BOB, as it was known to its some of its fans) melded a new spirit to "encompass health and weight consciousness" and a realization that the nation was made up of underappreciated regional cuisines such as Cajun-Creole and Tex-Mex. Originally launched as the Brick Oven Bistro in Boise, Idaho, in 1984, the residents of the Capital Hill neighborhood—and soon all of Denver—made the Brick Oven Beanery the city's own.

Referred to by an owner as "eclectic collection of Mom's home cooking," the BOB was a forerunner of "fast, casual," a marketing concept driving today's restaurant industry. The menu featured a $4.95 platter of beef, turkey, or ham with coleslaw or salad, hand-mashed potatoes, sage nut dressing, and whole wheat or French bread. The restaurant emphasized slowing down and enjoying food. It was too good to last, as the Brick Oven Beanery closed after a decade. In making the decision to close in the summer of 1995, owner Ed Hoagland found that "[i]t was no longer a great location…At lunch we'd have Cadillacs and Mercedes-Benz in our parking lot; for dinner, it'd be just about empty." The Brick Oven Beanery is gone, leaving only memories of many good meals and a business plan and menu worth re-creating.[187]

CHAPTER 6

The Check Please and Where Do We Eat from Here?

By the 2010s, new faces, new tastes, and greater awareness of good food could not be missed on cable television, in magazines, and in the restaurants we patronized. Denver's chefs did not solely blaze this trail, but the city's diners benefitted from these trends. Conversely, Denver's old guard restaurants are fading from the scene. Our story closes with an epitaph for those chefs, owners, and restaurateurs who got out when the getting was good. Or bad.

THOUGHT FOR FOOD

In a corner of Centennial where all the street names are the same and converge in a stew of Ways, Courts, and Circles, there lives a man who kept many of the restaurants mentioned over the previous five chapters in oranges, onions, and cabbage for most of the last century.

In 2014, Lou Mozer turned ninety. The chronometer means nothing, as he recalls the smallest detail of restaurants long forgotten over the past eight decades. Mozer was born in 1924 in Denver's Beth Israel Hospital, and at ten, he joined the family business, the Grand Junction Fruit Company at 420 15th Street. "You are tall enough to reach the scale, and you can count to twelve. You can go to work and help on weekends" is how the father-son job interview went. Father Sam Mozer and his brother-in-law, Nate

Markets like Grand Junction Fruit Company on 15th Street kept the city's restaurants supplied with fruits and vegetables for much of the twentieth century. *From Lou Mozer.*

Cohen, supplied fruit and produce to the city's restaurants. "We began with breakfast at The Manhattan nearly every day," and then it was off to take orders or deliver produce. Along 15th Street, Mozer's customers included Solomon's Grill, the Waffle House, Nettie's Bar and Grill, Have a Lunch, and the University Café. All gone.[188]

By the time he was fifteen, Mozer was doing a man's job. At six feet and two hundred pounds, he was already a more substantial presence than most men are in their thirties. Despite his size, collecting on accounts was sometimes difficult. "I would try to collect from Herb Wong at the New China Café, and he would come back out with a cleaver,"[189] Mozer laughed.

Mozer kept the many of the restaurants described in this book supplied. From his kitchen table, he observed, "Everybody wants to eat and run now. In the days of the Quorum or Le Profile, dinners were three- to four-hour deals."[190]

From behind his microphone, and involved in Denver's ever-changing dining landscape, Warren Byrne sees how mass media has lifted the culinary aspirations of Denver and other American cities. "The cooking channels on cable have made big names out of chefs. Thirty or forty years ago, if you

When the dream ends. It was Si's Bar-B-Que, GuadalaHarry's, and Gordo's. As of 2014, it is an empty lot. *Photo by Robert Autobee.*

went to your parents and told them you wanted to be a chef, they would have smacked upside your head."[191]

The January 14, 2014 edition of the city's surviving daily, the *Denver Post*, ran a front-page story examining the recent explosion of the city's new restaurants, as well as the pratfalls the majority face when customers don't show up. Headlined "Foodie Gold Rush," the paper went on to describe the glut of gastronomy in the Mile High City. Dining is increasingly importantly to a city and state dependent on tourism. Denver's "economic health is tied to the success of its dining scene." In 2012, 48 percent of downtown's sales tax, or about $18 million, came from restaurants—up from $16.4 million in 2011.[192]

Byrne cited regulations, liquor licensing, sexual harassment in the workplace, theft, and the myriad other bear traps waiting to prevent restaurants from achieving long and happy lives. A difficulty in stimulating a local style of cuisine is a growing population moving from elsewhere. Newcomers mostly want what they left behind. If that doesn't work, they will want the same piece of meat wrapped in cheese and bacon they could find in San Angelo, Texas, or Sacramento, California. "Chains have advertising clout," Byrne noted. "Mom and pops are at a disadvantage."[193]

Another concern is how technology affects one of the best aspects of dining: mood and ambience. Byrne noted, "With your iPad or phone, you can order your meal at some restaurants before you walk through the door.

Main Dining Room
NEW CHINA CAFE
726-32 E. Colfax Ave.
Denver, Colo.

The correspondent on the back of this postcard for the New China Café noted that it "had ice cream with wine on it" and that "you can take your bones home with you and make soup for the next day." *From authors' collection.*

People want control. They want to design their own meals." The memories associated with a happy event at a favorite place are giving way to parents and children going in different directions and barely stopping for meals together. Byrne lamented that dining out, in most cases, "is not special anymore."[194]

From Morgan's in the Desert, La Quinta, California, Jimmy Schmidt concurred that a dining memory isn't always about the food. "Great food memories activate as many senses as possible. Both the best and the worst. Do you remember what you had three weeks ago Tuesday? No, but you will remember what you have if the whole experience was a good one."[195]

For Rob Mohr, the restaurant business is "a big gamble," and hard work pays off only for a chosen few. "Not everybody loses money. The people who ran Victoria Station made tons and tons of money for fifteen years. Then you look around and think, 'I have $5 million in the bank. I'm forty-five. You might as well go out and enjoy it."[196] In Mohr's opinion, Denver was a great restaurant town decades ago. Now he finds that the scene has gotten "over sophisticated."

Holly Arnold Kinney of The Fort agreed, but she also foresees an intriguing time ahead: "Denver has always attracted brilliant people…Denver as a restaurant town may have been better in the 1950s and 1960s with very traditional mom and pop restaurants and good Japanese and Chinese. The city is now a little more cosmopolitan…Denver is recognized as a city where you can make your way as a chef."[197]

Tom Wilscam also sees many good meals before all of us: "Denver used to be a crappy restaurant town. Now it's damn good. Boulder is one of the top restaurant cities in the country."[198] We are left to consider, then, whether this generation of restaurants will provide memories similar to those over the past century.

The 2010s have been hard on north Denver's legendary red sauce restaurants. Three Sons started the exodus by transplanting west to Arvada. Longo's Subway Tavern at 3759 Lipan Street closed in 2012 after fifty-two years in the business, only to be followed down memory lane by Pagliacci's and Carbone's Meat Market. The long-pending sale of Lechuga's on 35th and Tejon hangs over the neighborhood.

The Grandinetti family came to Denver in the 1890s. It took another five decades, and Frank Grandinetti meeting Thelma Balzano over fruits and vegetables at a stand in lower downtown Denver, before getting into the restaurant business. Frank and Thelma opened Pagliacci's in a converted house on West 33rd Avenue in 1946. Thelma sold Pagliacci's to her sister Rose in 1977. Rose's son, Mark Langston-Gonzales, subsequently kept the sixty-six-year-old restaurant in the family until 2012. Langston-Gonzales stated, "I starting rolling meatballs here when I was ten years old, and now I'm running the place."

The restaurant went through hard times in the 1980s. Like so many others, it survived by bringing family in to help cook, serve, and clean. No one in the family was waiting to take over after the 2008 recession. In closing Pagliacci's in August 2012, Langston-Gonzales felt a small victory in avoiding "Americanizing" the menu. He knows the irony of when the restaurant opened in the late 1940s—the menu's left side featured southern fried chicken facing veal escallopine on the right. The new demographics in a changing north Denver forced the possibility of turning the family business into something Langston-Gonzales wanted to avoid: "Olive Garden ruined it for everybody. It is the Walmart of restaurants. I didn't want to go down that path."[199]

Now, as a real estate agent, Langston-Gonzales sees north Denver changing more every day. In his experience, the neighborhood began to lose its character as far back as the 1950s, when the second generation of Italian Americans with money "moved up the hill" and settled in suburbs like Wheat Ridge and Arvada. His heart and contacts remain in north Denver: "When

Time had the last laugh on the clown. Pagliacci's left the scene in 2012. *From Tom Noel Photo Collection, Auraria Library, AUR-3007.*

I tell clients, 'Let's go look at places in north Denver,' they say, 'I don't want to go to Thornton.'"[200]

We focused on those who fought the good fight and left behind gastronomic good feelings. One Denver restaurant still in business can trace its origins to a bar called the Black Cat, established in the 1890s. The story of Patsy's Inn reads like a family saga, with neighborhood wise guys, family spats, and the recipes for grandma's sauce all kept inside one man's head.

Ron Cito is related to Michael and Maggie Tolve Aiello, who turned the Black Cat pool hall and bar into the Italian Village. Michael Aiello's Black Cat was on Navajo Street in the 1890s and became a restaurant after Colorado's 1916 prohibition of alcohol. Ron's Aunt Maggie Aiello started the restaurant at its current location in about 1921. In the 1940s, her son George "Chubby" Aiello renamed it Patsy's Inn. It seemed like a good move as the nation entered the Second World War to associate with an ally, and the Irish looked like a good bet. As Chubby Aiello later reasoned, "We decided to make a name change and Patsy's Inn was born—overnight, we were Irish!" Patsy's Inn can make the claim that it is the oldest continuously operating Italian restaurant in the city.

North Denver's current reality of new people and businesses equals higher taxes. A slow drive through neighborhood streets clogged with construction

Renamed in the 1940s, Patsy's holds on as a north Denver bastion of spaghetti and lasagna. *Photo by Robert Autobee.*

equipment is the first indication that the old ways are fading. Now in his seventies, Cito, an electrician for most of his life, moved as quickly as he could when an opportunity to get back into the family restaurant fell his way. "This is a gift given from God. I feel that my Aunt Maggie or somebody in the family wanted this to come back to us." The days can be long, and sometimes Cito and his wife, Kimmie DeLancey-Cito, forget to eat. "It'll be ten o'clock, and the restaurant closed at nine." They'll often close a long day with a late dinner at another restaurant.[201]

Ethnic enclaves forming the long-standing gastronomic foundation of north Denver weren't the only parts of the Front Range to recently feel the cold blasts of change. Another fallen monument to how times and tastes change was Emil-Lene's Steak House at 16000 Smith Road in the wilds of Aurora. Metropolitan Denver today looks nothing like it did in 1959, but a person had to want a steak pretty badly to take their Escalante or Element out to Emil-Lene's nearly fifty years later. Too hokey, too old of a loyal customer base, and too high priced for some—and with a tree growing in the middle of the dining room—Emil-Lene's went out of business in early

Gone for nearly two decades, many Denverites recall good times at Little Pepina's at 3400 Osage. *From Tom Noel Photo Collection, Auraria Library, AUR-3010.*

2014. Twenty-one violations of the Tri-County health code in November 2013 didn't help.[202]

In 1959, restaurants survived on positive reviews and customers who kept coming back. A half century later, websites like Facebook, Yelp, and Menuism are turning everybody into a Mimi Sheraton kind of reviewer. Venturing into cyberspace, newcomers were merciless to Emil-Lene's cardboard cutout of John Wayne at the front door, the servers who recited the menu, and the price of sirloin—even the four-foot-high pepper mill (perhaps the funniest prop in Denver restaurant history) was unspared.

A New England transplant who came west in 1976, John Lehndorff soon found himself immersed in the Boulder food scene. During his career, he has prepped, cooked, and served. He also wrote and commentated as a food critic for two daily newspapers, two weeklies, and a local radio station. For Lehndorff, the current generation of newcomers to the Denver metro area has taken the strip malls and holes-in-the-walls and built on the story started on Larimer Street and in north Denver: "Aurora is filled with ethnic places. The owner speaks very little English, but any sons or cousins can translate. You find this in restaurants where the food comes from the Sudan, Eretria, Guatemala."[203]

The last observation belongs to Mrs. Ruth Bradford of Denver. At 102, she has seen nearly all of Denver's restaurant and service industry from her days as a carhop at the Oasis Drive In to Keeble's Sandwich Shop to Joe "Awful" Coffee's Ringside Lounge to running her mother's place, Bennett's Café. When asked what's different between dining out now and three-quarters of a century ago, she replied, "The way they dress now. If you had a speck of dirt on your uniform, you would be sent home."[204]

As we mentioned at the beginning, Denver may not rank in the minds of others as one of the great dining destinations on planet Earth. However, there are enough memories of good times, hardworking people, and memorable meals to rival any other city. Denver's first wave of dining establishments—from the 1870s Delmonico of the West to the 1890s The Manhattan—exist only as newspaper ads and menus in library collections. The invasion of the Victoria Stations and 94th Aero Squadrons have been pushed aside in the recollections of most longtime residents by the much-missed Normandy, White Spot, and Denver Drumstick. Denver in the second decade of the twenty-first century is

"Big Ruth" Bradford (left) and "Little Ruth" Bennett ran the Bennett Café in the 1950s. The Café was one of hundreds of lunch counters that kept Denver's working people going. *From Rose Ann Taht.*

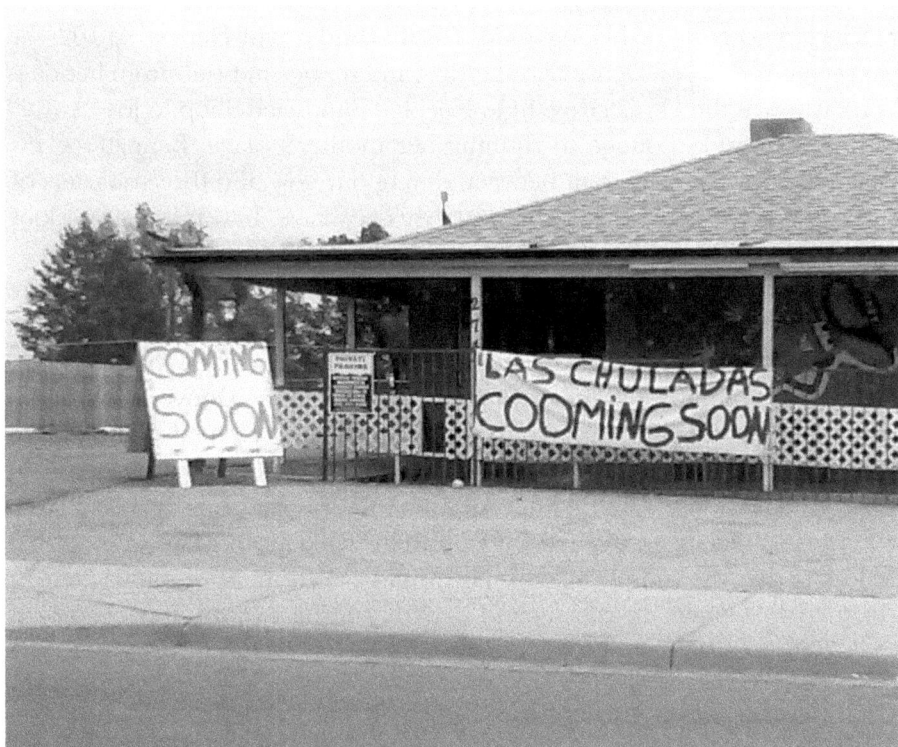

A restaurant remains the nearest, yet biggest, dream for the small businessperson. You cannot fault these new entrepreneurs' enthusiasm before they opened their restaurant in the spring of 2014. *From authors' collection.*

going through another cycle of great change. *Local, organic,* and *seasonal* are the words and sensations of the moment, again.

Those paid to keep track of these things—food critics, distributors, and accountants—all admit that they cannot keep up with the number of places that open, and close, in any given week. The adventurous are fortunate to be around as the city enters this new phase. However, let us hope that the old favorites are not leftovers as we savor this current chapter of Denver's dining history.

Notes

Introduction

1. Interview with John Lehndorff, April 23, 2014.
2. The authors wish to thank Nichole Goodman and Rob Mohr for reminiscing about these restaurants.
3. *Westword*, "Heaven on a Plate," January 11, 1980, 9.
4. U.S. Works Progress Administration, Colorado Records, "Colorado Eats," WH 2212, Western History Collection, Denver Public Library.

Chapter 1

5. Chauncey Thomas, "Some Characteristics of Jim Baker," *Colorado Magazine* 4, no. 4 (1927): 142.
6. Isabella L. Bird, *Life in the Rocky Mountains* (New York: G.P. Putman's Sons, 1880), 155–56.
7. J.F. Wharton, *The City of Denver from Its Earliest Settlement to the Present Time* (Denver, Colorado Territory: Byers & Dailey, 1866), 9.
8. Jerome C. Smiley, *History of Denver* (Denver: Times-Sun Publishing Company, 1901), 245; *Rocky Mountain News*, April 23 and 26, 1859.
9. *Rocky Mountain News*, April 26, 1859, 4.
10. Wharton, *City of Denver*, 15.
11. Mary Dorsey Sanford, "Across the Plains to Denver in 1860," *The Echo* 3, no. 9 (October 1925): 6.
12. Parker and Huyett, *The Illustrated Miner's Hand-Book and Guide to Pikes Peak, with a Reliable Map Showing All the Routes, and the Gold Regions of Western Kansas & Nebraska* (St. Louis, MO, 1859), 39.

13. Libeus Barney, *Letters Reminiscent of Pioneer Days in the West* (Denver: A.J. Ludditt Press, 1930). The quotes in this chapter are from letters dated May 7, July 12, October 4, and November 23, 1859.

14. Thomas J. Noel, *The City and the Saloon: Denver, 1858–1916* (Lincoln: University of Nebraska Press, 1982), 4.

15. Noel, *City and the Saloon*, 3–4; Lyle W. Dorsett, *The Queen City: A History of Denver* (Boulder, CO: Pruett Publishing Company, 1986), 27–29.

16. Louis L. Simonin, *The Rocky Mountain West in 1867*, translated by Wilson O Clough (Lincoln: University of Nebraska Press, 1966), 33.

17. *Rocky Mountain News*, July 14, 1866, 4.

18. Ibid., December 31, 1869, 4.

19. The sometimes conflicting bits of the Charpiot story are found in Thomas J. Noel, *Denver's Larimer Street* (Denver: Historic Denver Inc., 1981), 110; Maria Davies McGrath, "Men Who Arrived in What Is Now Colorado Prior to February 26, 1861," Document Division, Denver Museum Collection, n.d.; Ancestry.com, including "New York, Passenger Lists, 1820–1957"; "Iowa, State Census Collection, 1836–1925"; "Iowa, Select Marriages, 1809–1992"; "U.S. City Directories, 1821–1989"; "1870 United States Federal Census"; and "1900 United States Federal Census."

20. Parker & Huyett, *Illustrated Miner's Hand-Book*, 38–41; Steamboat Arabia Museum website, http://steamboatarabiamuseum.blogspot.com/2010/09/baltimore-cove-oysters-02.html.

21. A quick, unscientific survey of twenty-first-century Denver restaurants revealed very little oyster creativity, as modern diners settle for raw, fried, au gratin, Rockefeller, in gumbo, charbroiled, or occasionally on an omelet called the Hangtown Fry, at the recently opened Humbolt at 1700 Humbolt Street.

22. *Colorado Sun*, "The Restaurants of Denver: Where You Can Buy a Dinner for Fifteen Dollars and One for Fifteen Cents," January 17, 1892, 16; Mark Kurlansky, *The Big Oyster: History on the Half Shell* (New York: Balantine Books, 2006).

23. *Rocky Mountain News*, September 1, 1863, 3.

24. Forbes Parkhill, *Mister Barney Ford: A Portrait in Bistre* (Denver: Sage Books, 1963), 117–24, 140.

25. *Rocky Mountain News*, November 8, 1865, 1.

26. Ibid., July 1, 1867, 4.

27. Ibid., July 21, 1866, 1.

28. Lee Jacobs Carlin, "Sweet Magic: One Hundred Years of Baur's Restaurant," *Colorado Heritage* (Spring 2002): 15.

29. *Denver Times*, "Old Arcade on Junk Pile…," November 9, 1918, 3.

30. *Denver Republican*, February 1, 1891, 8.

31. *La Patria*, December 15, 1891, 4.

32. *Denver Times*, November 17, 1902, Sec. 2, 10.

33. Louis Simonin noted that Overland Mail coaches could travel 110 to 115 miles per day. He left Paris by ship on September 13, 1867, and arrived nine days later in New York. The train to Chicago took about thirty-six hours and about that

again to Julesburg, Colorado. Leaving Julesburg on the evening of October 2, his stage arrived in Denver around midnight on October 3, 1867.

34. Ira De Augustine Reid, *The Negro Population of Denver, Colorado: A Survey of Its Economic and Social Status* (Denver: Denver Inter-racial Commission, 1929), 44. We hope that descendants of those named in this chapter will add to the resources available at the Blair-Caldwell Library, the Western History Department of the Denver Public Library, or the Stephen H. Hart Library at History Colorado.

35. Steven Hart Library, History Colorado, Microfilm, Misc. W939i, Writers' Program of the Work Projects Administration in the State of Colorado, "Negro Pioneers: Interview with John Henry Lewis," circa 1940.

36. Ancestry.com, "U.S. City Directories, 1821–1989."

37. Gerald E. Rudolph, "The Chinese in Colorado, 1869–1911," master's thesis, University of Denver, 1964, 104–6.

38. U.S. Works Progress Administration, Colorado Records, "America Eats," WH 2212, Western History Collection, Denver Public Library.

39. Interview with Ruth Bradford, June 17, 2014; *Rocky Mountain News*, "Again Ill-Luck Closes Manhattan Restaurant," July 29, 1950, 26.

CHAPTER 2

40. Interview with Carl Cerveny, January 15, 2014.

41. *Rocky Mountain News*, "Monument Recalls Pell's Restaurant," September 7, 1958, 51.

42. Ibid., "Onion Rings Got Rolling," April 30, 2000, 6-A.

43. *Denver Times*, "Fight Over Color Line," March 9, 1903, 4.

44. Ibid.

45. *Denver Jewish News*, December 27, 1923, 2.

46. *Denver Post*, "Famed Denver Café Will Close Doors," April 20, 1941, 1.

47. *Colorado Statesman*, April 25, 1941, 2.

48. *Denver Times*, "Boycott Declared on Japanese Restaurants," July 24 1901, 10; *Denver Times*, "No More Boycotts on Restaurants," July 8, 1902.

49. *Denver Times*, "Odds and Ends," October 24, 1902, 16.

50. *Colorado Sun*, "The Restaurants of Denver: Where You Can Buy a Dinner for Fifteen Dollars and One for Fifteen Cents," January 17, 1892, 16.

51. *Denver Republican*, "Girl Strikers Picket the Restaurant They Left," February 10, 1902, 6.

52. *Rocky Mountain News*, "Public Scrambles Over Food," May 14, 1903, 2.

53. David Brundage, *The Making of Western Labor Radicalism: Denver's Organized Workers, 1878–1905* (Urbana: University of Illinois Press, 1994), 146–47; *Denver Times*, "All Denver Rejoices Over the Happy Ending of the Labor Strike," May 30, 1903, 1.

54. Forrest H. Johnson, *Denver's Old Theater Row: The Story of Curtis Street and Its Glamorous Show Business* (Denver: Gem Publications, 1970), 36; *Rocky Mountain Business Journal*, "Lusky: Memories of Edelweiss Café," January 2, 1980, Sec. 1, 2.

55. Moya Hansen, "Entitled to Full and Equal Enjoyment: Leisure and Entertainment in the Denver Black Community, 1900–1930," 34–35,

seminar paper, with original held at Stephen H. Hart Library, History Colorado, Denver.

56. Carlin, "Sweet Magic," 15.

57. Johnson, *Denver's Old Theater Row*, 36; interview with Ruth Bradford, June 17, 2014.

58. Johnson, *Denver's Old Theater Row*, 32.

59. *Denver Municipal Facts* (City and County of Denver) 1, no. 4 (June 1918): 17.

60. Ibid. 1, no. 10, "About Unescorted Women" (April 24, 1909): 7.

61. Ibid. 4, no. 13, "Vocal Solos in Cafés" (March 30, 1912): 6.

62. *Denver Directory, 1940* (Denver: Gazetteer Company Inc., 1940), 285.

63. *Denver Times*, "Queer Food Concoctions: Dishes in Darkest Denver," January 12, 1902, 19.

64. Ibid.

65. Interview with Nancy Brueggeman, April 17, 2014.

66. *Rocky Mountain News*, "Tearoom Boasts Recipes that Stood the Test of Time," March 15, 1987, 18.

67. *Ballenger & Richards Denver Directory, 1922* (Denver: Gazetteer Publishing & Printing Company, 1922), 1,115.

68. *The Echo*, "Eating in Five Languages in Denver" (December 1925): 4.

69. Ibid.

70 *Rocky Mountain News*, "It's Fascinating Work to Operate Restaurant Like Casa Rosa de Oro," August 1, 1943, 25.

71. Ibid.

72. *The Echo* (May 1925): 11.

73. Ibid., "Eating in Five Languages in Denver," 4.

74. U.S. Works Progress Administration, "Colorado Racial Groups in Denver, 1936–1942—Greeks," WH 2212, Western History Collection, Denver Public Library.

75. U.S. Bureau of the Census, Fourteenth Census of the United States, vol. 2, "Population, 1920" (Washington, D.C.: Government Printing Office, 1922), 47; U.S. Bureau of the Census, Fifteenth Census of the United States, vol. 2, "Population, 1930" (Washington, D.C.: Government Printing Office, 1932), 23; U.S. Bureau of the Census, Sixteenth Census of the United States, "Population, 1940," vol. 2, "Characteristics of the Population" (Washington, D.C.: Government Printing Office, 1943), part 1, 629, 636, 657, 787; part 5, 1,041; part 6, 1,026, 1,044, 1,053; part 7, 400.

76. *Colorado Statesman*, June 24, 1911, 1; *Ballenger & Richards Thirty-ninth Annual Denver City Directory for 1911* (Denver: Ballenger & Richards, 1911).

77. *Colorado Statesman*, May 15, 1915, 5.

78. *The Echo*, "Eating in Five Languages in Denver," 5.

79. *Colorado Statesman*, December 22, 1940.

CHAPTER 3

80. *Denver Post*, "Dorothy Ballast Jarrett, Who Ran the Drive-In with the First Cheeseburgers, Dies at 94," March 20, 2011, Sec. A, 20.

81. *Rocky Mountain News Sunday Spotlight Magazine*, "Two Recipes for Rockybilt Hamburger Sauce," June 22, 1997, Sec. D, 7.

82. *Rocky Mountain News*, "Hamburger Haven Closes Its Doors," July 25, 1969, 58. The authors thank Karen Zoltenko for her memories of Hi's Hamburgs.

83. Colorado Emergency Relief Administration, "Social Welfare in Colorado," *Bulletin on Social Statistics* 2, no. 4 (July, August and September, 1935): 3–4.

84. Ibid.

85. Colorado Visitors Bureau, *Where to Eat in Colorado*, circa 1958.

86. *Denver Post*, "Rockybilt Chief Doesn't Count Cost of 5-Cent Burger Fling," July 17, 1951, 18.

87. Ibid.

88. *Cervi's Business Journal*, "Not Books, but Hamburgers to Occupy Library Site," May 20, 1954, 2.

89. *Westword*, "Some Tremendous Take-Outs," March 31, 1978, 20.

90. *Rocky Mountain News*, "Say Cheese for Burger Anniversary," March 6, 1987, 84.

91. *Rocky Mountain News Sunday Magazine*, "Bringing Manners to Micky's," October 18, 1992, Sec. M, 16–17.

92. *Westword*, "No Micky Mouse Deal," November 23, 2000, 67.

93. *Denver Post*, "Bay Was North Star in Wrestling," July 11, 2012, Sec. B, 2.

94. *Denver Combined Suburban Directory* (Englewood, CO: XL Directory Service, 1952), 61–62.

95. Interview with Carl Cerveny, January 15, 2014.

96. Scotchman Motor Restaurants website, http://www.scotchmanreunion.org/album/pages/HPIM0122_JPG.html; *Westword*, "Scotchman Closes," October 13, 1977, 3.

97. Interview with Carl Cerveny, January 15, 2014.

98. Ibid.

99. Ibid.

100. Ibid.

101. *Rocky Mountain News*, "Golden Goose Fine for Lunch," May 19, 1972, 89.

102. *Denver Business Journal*, "Round the Corner Tests New Franchise Concept," September 28, 1992, 12.

103. *Rocky Mountain News*, "Parent of 'Sliders & Nails' Files Chapter 11 Petition," September 7, 1983, 88.

104. *Denver Post*, "Pasta, Pepperoni, Provolone and Pride," March 19, 1975, Sec. AA, 9.

105. Interview with Ron Cito and Kimmie DeLancey-Cito, June 9, 2014.

106. Interview with Nick and Kathleen Andurlakis, June 2, 2014.

CHAPTER 4

107. *The Gazetteer Company's Denver (Denver County, Colo) City Directory*, vol. 71 (Denver: Gazetteer Company, 1945), 1,888; *The Gazetteer Company's Denver (Denver County, Colo) City Directory*, vol. 72 (Denver: Gazetteer Company, 1947), 2,358; Greg Robinson, *After Camp: Portraits in Midcentury Japanese American Life and Politics* (Oakland: University of California Press, 2012), 48–49.

108. *Denver Post*, "Gov't Raps City Café Sanitation," November 26, 1947, 1, 24; *Denver Post*, "Denver's Restaurants Get High Health Rating," March 20, 1955, Sec. A, 19; interview with Ruth Bradford and Rose Ann Taht, June 17, 2014.

109. The Tiffin menu, circa 1950, from authors' collection.

110. Interview with Marta Gonzàlez and Gregorio Alcaro, January 25, 2014.

111. Ibid.

112. Denver Restaurants, A–C, "Mexican Specialties," Clipping File, Western History Collection, Denver Public Library.

113. Interview with Marta Gonzàlez and Gregorio Alcaro, January 25, 2014.

114. Ibid.; *Denver Magazine*, "Buen Apetito: From Denver's Mexican Food Loving Celebs," (September 1977): 34.

115. Interview with Marta Gonzàlez and Gregorio Alcaro, January 25, 2014.

116. Ibid.

117. *Rocky Mountain News*, "Lund's Restaurant Closes Saturday," February 27, 1970, 83; *Denver Post*, "Pancake Purveyor Was Blunt but Sweet," February 4, 2007, Sec. C, 6.

118. *Rocky Mountain News*, "Duffy's Shamrock Restaurant Founder Dies," January 28, 1992, 11; *Denver Post*, "Duffy's Last Call," November 15, 2006, Sec. B, 1.

119. *Rocky Mountain News*, "Ah, that Chinese Cooking!" May 3, 1948, 19; Menu Collection, WH1509, Western History Collection, Denver Public Library.

120. *Rocky Mountain News*. "Howard: Fun Place to Hang Out," http://m. rockymountainnews.com/news/2009/feb27/howard-fun-place-to-hang-out.

121. Linda Ruth Harvey, Jenny Von Hoehenstraeten and Mary Jo Fostina, eds., *Colorado Gourmet Gold: Cookbook of Recipes from Popular Colorado Eateries* (Denver: Laika Inc., 1980), Chapter II, page 5.

122. *Denver Catholic Register*, July 28, 1978, 16.

123. Tillie Lowrey, *Historic Denver Restaurant Recipes* (Wonderful World of Palaad, LLC Kindle, 2012); *Rocky Mountain Business Journal*, February 18, 1976, 37.

124. *Denver Post*, "New Denver Restaurant Has Gallic Atmosphere," March 6, 1952, 43.

125. Lou Mozer, "A Colorado Food Historian's Story Part Six," *Restaurant News of the Rockies* (July 2011), 1.

126. Pierre Wolfe, *Tastefully Yours: Savoring Denver's Restaurant Past* (Denver: Professional Book Center, 2002), 65.

127. Mozer, "Colorado Food Historian's Story Part Six," 1.

128. *Denver Post*, "$250,000 Seafood Café Set," December 11, 1960, Sec. E, 1; Wolfe, *Tastefully Yours*, 65.

129. *Denver Post*, "$250,000 Seafood Café Set," 1.

130. Ibid., March 7, 1966, 3; and March 25, 1966, 31.

131. *Rocky Mountain News*, "A Matter of Taste," *Now* section, December 21, 1975, 21.

132. Ibid., "Lafitte Restaurant Sued in Flap Over $16,000," December 30, 1983, 14.

133. Beverly Anderson Nemiro and Donna Miller Hamilton, *Colorado a La Carte*, Series 2 (Denver: Sage Books, 1966), 113.

134. *Rocky Mountain News Sunday Magazine*, "Last Course," April 22, 1990, Sec. M, 15.

135. Ibid., 16.

136. *Denver Post*, "Normandy's Owners Say Adieu," June 2, 2000, Sec. C, 2.

137. Papers of Pierre Wolfe, WH1465, Western History Collection, Denver Public Library. This recipe has variations; see the Epicurious website, http://www.epicurious.com/recipes/food/views/Roast-Five-Spice-Duck-with-Honeyed-Mango-Chutney-Sauce-103911.

138. Menu Collection, WH1509, Western History Collection, Denver Public Library.

139. *Denver Post*, "Too Many Chickens Created Denver's Drumsticks," April 7, 1964, 39.

140. Recipe Link website, http://www.recipelink.com/msgbrd/board_14/2004/MAY/14273.html.

141. *Denver Post*, "White Spot Is for Pilgrims of Late, Late Scene," August 18, 1964, 28.

142. *Cervi's Business Journal*, September 4, 1974, Sec. 1, 8.

143. *Rocky Mountain News*, "He Has Bright Idea for White Spots," October 13, 1968, 58.

144. *Denver Post*, "Hippies Picket Café, Claim 'Discrimination,'" August 16, 1969, 26.

145. Ibid., "Restaurant Backed in Non-Bias Ouster," August 8, 1969, 2.

146. Ibid., "Lights Out at the White Spot," June 26, 2001, Sec. C, 1, 3.

147. Ibid.

148. Billie Arlene Grant, *Daddy Bruce Randolph: The Pied Piper of Denver* (Aurora, CO: Accent Advantage, 1986), 55, 70.

149. *Denver Post*, "Sculpture of Denver's 'Daddy Bruce' Saved from Trash," November 15, 2009, B-1.

150. Interview with Peggy Nelson, May 11, 2014.

151. *Rocky Mountain News*, "Restaurant Cooks Up Tradition," March 25, 1990, Sec. B, 5.

152. Ibid.

Chapter 5

153. Interview with Tom Wilscam, January 24, 2014.

154. Nemiro and Hamilton, *Colorado a la Carte*, 63.

155. *Denver Post*, "Take a Whopping Appetite to the Hungry Farmer," October 13, 1964, 55.

156. Ibid.

157. Sam Arnold, *Sam Arnold's Feast of Life* (Denver: Fur Press, 1974), 3; *Denver Magazine* (July 1976): 25.

158. *Denver Magazine* (July 1976): 25.

159. Ibid.

160. *Rocky Mountain News*, "City, Wellshire Settle Utility Bill," July 31, 1982, 7.

161. Ibid.

162. Jane Stern and Michael Stern, *The Lexicon of Real American Food* (Guilford, CT: Lyons Press, 2011), 274; *Rocky Mountain News Sunday Magazine*, "Old Dutch Mill Landmark of Night Life in 1920s," April 17, 1982, Sec. N, 18–19.

163. *Denver Post*, "Yum Yum Tree Offers 302 Different Dishes," June 30, 1968, Sec. J, 4.

164. Ibid., "Making a Memorable Menu: Yum Yum!" n.d.

165. *Rocky Mountain News*, "Landmark Restaurant Gone," February 25, 1990, 6.

166. Ibid., "Golden Goose Fine for Lunch," May 19, 1972, 88–89; *Rocky Mountain News*, "Don't Be Fooled by the Exterior," February 4, 1972, 86.

167. Stern and Stern, *Lexicon*, 275.

168. Interview with Tom Wilscam, January 24, 2014.

169. Interview with Holly Arnold Kinney, February 24, 2014.

170. *Jefferson Sentinel*, April 2, 1964, 19.

171. Ibid., "Let's Start at 440," April 1, 1973, 29.

172. *Denver Post*, "Rosalie's Serves Fried Chicken Like the Old Days," February 28, 1967, 26.

173. *Rocky Mountain News*, "Zuider Zee Restaurant Opens Here," September 8, 1969, 74–76.

174. Denver city directories, 1970–75.

175. Interview with Nick and Kathleen Andurlakis, June 2, 2014.

176. *Westword*, "Elvis's Beloved Fool's Gold Loaf Sandwich Was Born in Denver," August 16, 2012, http://blogs.westword.com/cafesociety/2012/08/elvis_fools_gold_denver.php.

177. *LA Weekly*, "Q&A with Gustavo Arellano: Taco USA, Mexican Authenticity + Food Writing," April 9, 2012, http://www.laweekly.com/squidink/2012/04/09q-and-a-with-gustavo-arellano-taco-usa.

178. *Westword*, "Why Denver Is Home to the Best Mexican Dish in the United States," April 5, 2012, http://www.westword.com/2012-04-05/restaurants/denver-greatest-mexican-food-united-states.

179. *Colorado's Gourmet Gold* 14, no. 9; Arnold, *Sam Arnold's Feast of Life*, 9.

180. S.J. Guffey, "Critics' Choice: Reviewing the Reviewers," *Denver Magazine* (August 1986): S-9.

181. *Denver Post*, "Cooking in the Fast Lane," January 19, 1986, 10.

182. *Denver Magazine*, "Rattlesnake Strikes Fancy" (May 1986), 72; interview with Jimmy Schmidt, May 2, 2014.

183. Interview with Jimmy Schmidt, May 2, 2014.

184. Ibid.

185. Interview with John Lehndorff, April 23, 2014.

186. *New York Times*, "What's Doing in Denver," August 2, 1987, Sec. A, 10.

187. *Westword*, "Full of Beans," December 4, 1985, 35; *Denver Post*, "Colfax Fixture Beanery Missed," August 10, 1995, Sec. C, 1.

CHAPTER 6

188. Lou Mozer, "A Unique Food Historian Story in Denver & Colorado," *Restaurant News of the Rockies* (February 2011), 3.

189. Interview with Lou Mozer, January 24, 2014.

190. Ibid.

191. Interview with Warren Byrne, January 15, 2014.

192. *Denver Post*, "Foodie Gold Rush," January 14, 2014, Sec. A, 1, 7.

193. Interview with Warren Byrne, January 15, 2014.

194. Ibid.

195. Interview with Jimmy Schmidt, May 2, 2014.

196. Interview with Rob Mohr, April 18, 2014.

197. Interview with Holly Arnold Kinney, February 24, 2014.

198. Interview with Tom Wilscam, January 24, 2014.

199. Interview with Mark Langston-Gonzales, April 1, 2014.

200. Ibid.

201. Interview with Ron Cito and Kimmie DeLancey-Cito, June 9, 2014; http://www.patsysinn.com/patsysinn/history.html.

202. *Westword*, "Emil-Lene's Sirloin House, One of Denver's Cow Classics, Shutters After More than Fifty Years," March 20, 2014, http://blogs.westword.com/cafesociety/2014/03/emil-lenes_sirloin_house_closed_steak_house.php.

203. Interview with John Lehndorff, April 23, 2014.

204. Interview with Ruth Bradford, June 17, 2014. A special thank-you to Mrs. Bradford's daughter, Rose Ann Taht, for arranging a delightful talk with her mother.

Index

A

Admiral Restaurant 47
African Americans 9, 10, 23, 33, 36, 46, 50, 60, 61, 99, 110, 112
Aiello, George "Chubby" 140
Aiello, Michael and Maggie 140
Akebono 97
Alcaro, Gregorio 89, 90
Alpine Village Inn 114
Andurlakis, Nick and Kathleen 79, 125, 126
Aoki, Fred and Chiyeko 97
Apple Tree Shanty 97
Arcade Restaurant 30
Arellano, Gustavo 127
Arnold, Sam 90, 116

B

bakeries 14, 59
Ballast, Louis 64
Barney, Libeus 16
Barron, Joel 121
Baur, Otto 28
Baur's Restaurant 29, 41, 50
Bay, Ronnie 70, 71
Beebe, Lucius 87

Bennett's Café 84, 143
Bennett, Theron C. 118
Bird, Isabella 14
Black Cat. *See* Patsy's Inn
Blue Parrot 41
boarding houses 24, 33
Bradford, Ruth 39, 84, 143
Brick Oven Beanery 133
Broch, Lucien 98, 102
Brown, George and Rose Mary 99
Brueggeman, Nancy 55
Byrne, Warren 136

C

Calhoun, "Haystacks" 67
canoli/cannoli 62, 63, 78, 80
Capitol, the 18, 20
Carbone, Dominic 78
Carbone, Richard 79
Carbone's Italian Sausage House 78
Carbone's Meat Market 139
Carlin, Lee Jacobs 50
Carr, Governor Ralph 67
Carr's Hotel 25
Casa Mayan 87, 90
Casa Rosa de Oro 58

Catignani, Dario 33
Cerveny, Carl 72, 75
Chang, James 129
Charpiot, Frederick 18, 27, 146
Charpiot, Louis 18
Charpiot's Hotel Restaurant 31
Chas. Whipple & Company 25
cheeseburgers 64
Chesney, Roy 66, 68
Chez Michelle 103
chile rellenos 89, 91
chili parlor 53
Chinese Americans 9, 10, 33, 36, 93
Christopher, Herman 72
Chung, Mae 61
Cito, Ron and Kimmie 79, 140, 141
Clark, A.C. 27
Clements, Tony 110
Clements, William F. 108
Club Tivoli 130
Coffee, Joe "Awful" 81, 84, 143
Cole, James 27
Cole's Dance Hall 19
Colorado Mine Company 125
Coloroso, Dominic 70
Colwell, James 28
Condon's Café 31
Conner, Linda 74
Cork 'n' Cleaver 123
Crawford, Dana 98

D

Delmonico of the West 20
Denver Drumstick 105, 107, 119
Denver Dry Goods 54, 55
Disguez, Modesto 57
Dolman, Mr. and Mrs. Samuel 16
Douglass, Corky 103
Duffy, Bernard J. 92
Duffy's Shamrock 92

E

Edelweiss Café, The 39, 41, 43, 49, 50
Eisenhower, President Dwight D. 92

Elitch, John 30
El Nuevo Chapultepec 57
Emil-Lene's Steak House 141
Ethel's House of Soul 112

F

Fong, Bob 93
Fong, Esther and Frank 93
Fool's Gold sandwich 126
Ford, Barney 23, 34
Foster, Jack 93
Fred's Place 97
Frosted Scotchman 72, 74
Fuji En 96, 121

G

Gaetano's 63
Gerstle, Heinz 103
Ginn Mill 46
Golden Dragon 128
Golden Ox 123
Gonzàlez, Marta 87, 90
Gonzàlez, Ramon and Carolina 87
Goto, Leo 90, 113, 116
Grandinetti, Frank and Thelma 139
Grand Junction Fruit Company 135
Greek Americans 53, 59, 79
Greene, Peter 123

H

hamburgers 11, 50, 62, 63, 67, 68, 70,
   72, 75, 77, 128
Harding, Charles 46
Hawkins, Bud 120
Hermann, Karen 103
Hi's Hamburgs 68
Hotel Toscano 31
Howard, Michael Balfe 93
Humble, Henry 16
Humpty Dumpty Barrel Drive-In 64,
   70
Hungry Dutchman 116
Hungry Farmer 114

I

immigrants 33, 61, 91, 98, 100
Ingram, Billy 65
International Restaurant 18
Italian Americans 11, 31, 33, 59, 63,
79, 139
Italian Village. *See* Patsy's Inn

J

Japanese Americans 33, 36, 47, 67, 81,
90, 96, 116
Jefferson 440, the 122
Joe's Buffet 128
J. Zimmerlie Lunch Room 52

K

Karavites, M. 53
Karczewsky & Company 14
Karczewsky, Edward 14
Kinney, Holly Arnold 92, 121, 138
Kountze, Luther 23
Kreck, Dick 70

L

Lafitte's 98, 100
Lande's 123
Langston-Gonzales, Mark 139
Le Central 121
Lechuga's 63, 79
Lehndorff, John 8, 132, 142
Leo's Place 117
Le Profile 81, 136
Lewis, John Henry 36
Library, the 120
liverling 54
Lombardi, Frank and Ken 92
Longo's Subway Tavern 80, 139
Lotus Room 93
lunch counter 23, 51
Lund, John, Jr. 92
Lund, John, Sr. 91
Lund's Swedish Pancake House 91

M

Manhattan, The 39, 41, 43, 44, 46, 48,
52, 99, 121, 136, 143
Mansei-An 83
McNichols, William 117
McVittie, Albert and Bonnie 50
McVittie's 42, 50
M&D Café 112
Mexican Americans 33, 53, 57, 87,
90, 127
Meyers, Austin 105
Micky Manor 70, 71
Mister G's 123
Mohr, Rob 67, 138
Mon Petit 130
Morris, Jennifer 110
Mozer, Lou 135
Mrs. Rosen's Lunch Room 59
Mr. Steak 123
Muro, Tony 107
Murphy's Restaurant 10
Murphy, William E. 10

N

Nelson, Peggy 111
New China Café 136
New York Kosher Delicatessen and
Lunch Room 59
Nick's Café 77
94th Aero Squadron 118
Normandy 103

O

Occioni's 59
O'Hara, George 47
Old Dutch Mill 118
Old Mexico Chile & Coffee House
53
Oriental Restaurant 61
Out of Bounds 120
oysters 18, 20, 31, 43

P

Pagliacci's 139
Palace Bakery 48
Pappas, C.K. 53
Patio, the 100, 121
Patsy's Inn 79, 140
Peabody, Governor James 48
Pell, George W., Sr. 43
Pell's Oyster House 39, 41, 52
Peña, Federico 112
People's Restaurant 23
Pierre, Lawrence 111
Pierre's Supper Club 112
Pinhorn, Richard 45, 99, 121
Plummer, Hiram V. 68
Porter, Lavina 17
Pourdad, Frank 113, 130
Presley, Elvis 126
Prince Charlie's Fish and Chips 124

Q

Quorum, the 81, 100, 102, 110, 136

R

racism 10, 33, 46, 61, 87, 99, 109
Raffelock, David 57, 59
Randolph, "Daddy" Bruce 111
Rapp, Chris 39
Rattlesnake Club 130, 131
recipes
  Canoli 80
  Casserole Neptune 101
  Chicken à la King 55
  Chile Rellenos 89
  Denver Drumstick Gravy 107
  Honey Crisp Bananas or Apples 129
  Hot Kookie or Choking Coke 73
  Lotus Room Egg Rolls 94
  Mija Pie 29
  Mija Toffee Candy 30
  Rockybilt Hamburger Sauce 66
  Tante Louise's Roasted Five-Spiced
    Half Duck 104

Reed, Gertrude 58
Reithmann, John J. 25
Reitze, Henry 14
Rice, William A. 61
Ringside Lounge 81, 84, 143
Rockybilt 63, 66, 67, 68, 70, 71, 75, 77
Round the Corner 75

S

Sakura Square 83
Sanford, Mary Dorsey 15
Sasaki, Guy 36
Schaibly, August 47
Schmidt, Jimmy 113, 131, 138
Scotchman Motor Restaurant. *See*
    Frosted Scotchman
Scotch 'n' Sirloin 123
Scott, Annie 35
Scott, Buck and Cindy 125
Shank, Jean and Paul 87
Shaw's Drug Store 61
Sides, Harriet 35
Sidney's Fish and Chips 124
Simonin, Louis L. 17
Sky Chef 106
Sliders and Nails 77
Sperte, Joe 98, 100
Sperte, Roger 98
steaks 30, 33, 39, 45, 50, 81, 87, 102,
    121, 122, 141
Stern, Jane and Michael 118, 121
St. Louis Barbecue Inn 61
Suchotzki, Charles 49

T

Tabor, Baby Doe 39
Taht, Rose Ann 84
Tally Ho 122
Tante Louise 103
Taylor's Supper Club 108
Tiffin Inn 87
Tortoni's 42, 47
Trader Vic's 116
Trujillo, Manuel 58

U

Union Bakery Restaurant & Lager Beer
    Saloon, the 15

V

Victoria Station 120, 138

W

Wagner, H.O. 34
Warren, Bob 109
Wellshire Golf Course 117
Wharton, J.F. 14
White Peoples Chile Parlor 53
White Spot 105, 108
Wilscam, Tom 113, 124
Wilson, Billy 121
Wolfe, Pierre 81, 99, 100, 102, 121
Wong, Herb 136

Y

yeast 15
Yum Yum Tree 118

Z

Zoltenko, Karen 68

About the Authors

Coauthors and historians Robert and Kristen Autobee enjoy exploring Colorado's history together. Robert's ancestor Charles Autobees ventured to Colorado decades before the territory's first chile relleno. Robert admits that he probably ate at all the places mentioned from the fourth chapter onward to the book's conclusion. Robert's first book on Denver's past, *If You Stick with Barnum*, is part of the *Essays and Monographs in Colorado History* series published by the Colorado Historical Society. Previously a journalist for four Colorado newspapers, Robert has spent the past two decades as a historian for state and federal agencies and private firms. He currently researches and writes on topics as varied as mineral rights and architectural styles.

Kristen is a former collections curator and museum administrator who today works as a historical researcher for expert witnesses and other litigation projects. She arrived in Colorado in the 1990s and realized early on that Robert had good taste in restaurants—even the ones that looked scary. They met over a very loud jukebox at a historical society meeting and later found a quiet restaurant to get to know each other. She continues to write on local history topics when the time allows.

This is their second coauthored book.